Conversion of Military Enterprises

NATO ASI Series

Advanced Science Institutes Series

A Series presenting the results of activities sponsored by the NATO Science Committee, which aims at the dissemination of advanced scientific and technological knowledge, with a view to strengthening links between scientific communities.

The Series is published by an international board of publishers in conjunction with the NATO Scientific Affairs Division

A Life Sciences **B Physics**	Plenum Publishing Corporation London and New York
C Mathematical and Physical Sciences **D Behavioural and Social Sciences** **E Applied Sciences**	Kluwer Academic Publishers Dordrecht, Boston and London
F Computer and Systems Sciences **G Ecological Sciences** **H Cell Biology** **I Global Environmental Change**	Springer-Verlag Berlin, Heidelberg, New York, London, Paris and Tokyo

PARTNERSHIP SUB-SERIES

1. Disarmament Technologies	Kluwer Academic Publishers
2. Environment	Springer-Verlag / Kluwer Academic Publishers
3. High Technology	Kluwer Academic Publishers
4. Science and Technology Policy	Kluwer Academic Publishers
5. Computer Networking	Kluwer Academic Publishers

The Partnership Sub-Series incorporates activities undertaken in collaboration with NATO's Cooperation Partners, the countries of the CIS and Central and Eastern Europe, in Priority Areas of concern to those countries.

NATO-PCO-DATA BASE

The electronic index to the NATO ASI Series provides full bibliographical references (with keywords and/or abstracts) to more than 50000 contributions from international scientists published in all sections of the NATO ASI Series.
Access to the NATO-PCO-DATA BASE is possible in two ways:

– via online FILE 128 (NATO-PCO-DATA BASE) hosted by ESRIN, Via Galileo Galilei, I-00044 Frascati, Italy.

– via CD-ROM "NATO-PCO-DATA BASE" with user-friendly retrieval software in English, French and German (© WTV GmbH and DATAWARE Technologies Inc. 1989).

The CD-ROM can be ordered through any member of the Board of Publishers or through NATO-PCO, Overijse, Belgium.

Series 4: Science and Technology Policy – Vol. 10

Conversion of Military Enterprises

A Practical Approach of Industry and Science

edited by

Wolfgang G. Puppe
DOWC Ost-West-Consult GmbH,
Dresdner Bank Group,
Germany

Dmitriy V. Sergeev
Association of St. Petersburg,
Industrial Enterprises,
Russia

and

Albina I. Nikkonen
Regional Foundation for Science and Technology Development,
St. Petersburg, Russia

Kluwer Academic Publishers

Dordrecht / Boston / London

Published in cooperation with NATO Scientific Affairs Division

Proceedings of the NATO Advanced Research Workshop on
Conversion of Military Enterprises
A Practical Approach of Industry and Science
St. Petersburg, Russia
November 20–23, 1995

A C.I.P. Catalogue record for this book is available from the Library of Congress.

ISBN 0-7923-4342-5

Published by Kluwer Academic Publishers,
P.O. Box 17, 3300 AA Dordrecht, The Netherlands.

Kluwer Academic Publishers incorporates the publishing programmes of
D. Reidel, Martinus Nijhoff, Dr W. Junk and MTP Press.

Sold and distributed in the U.S.A. and Canada
by Kluwer Academic Publishers,
101 Philip Drive, Norwell, MA 02061, U.S.A.

In all other countries, sold and distributed
by Kluwer Academic Publishers Group,
P.O. Box 322, 3300 AH Dordrecht, The Netherlands.

Printed on acid-free paper

Printed in the Netherlands

Table of Contents

Introduction

Dear Reader,

Before you begin to study this book please be aware of the complexity of the "Conversion of Military Enterprises in Russia", The question of conversion is not only a change of the market and products it is in the former socialist and now "on the way of privatisation" - countries a complete reorganisation of the social structure and companies. In the past a performance of the Russian armaments' industry was a continual source of surprise to experts. It was obvious that apart from civilian industry there must be areas where important technological expertise had been created and built up. Since 5 years, conversion of military enterprise has been the principal topic of numerous conferences and studies. State institutions and international organisations can promote and accelerate the exchange of information and the restructuring process. However, the success of this process ultimately depends on how the economy will accept this change and how far market economy forces-can develop it. The NATO Advanced Research Workshop "Conversion of Military Enterprises in Russia- A Practical Approach of Industry and Science" was an excellent possibility for all participants from NATO-countries and from Russia, Ukraine and Belarus to discuss experiences and results after 5 years of reform period, All participating scientists noticed this aspect was proud to participate in this NATO event. Special thanks to professor Alan Jubier from the NATO Scientific and Environmental Affairs division for his engaged support to enable the possibility of holding this workshop Specific thanks for the cosponsoring and positive support by the Ministry of Science and Technnlogy policy of the Russian Federation and by the City of St. Petersburg itself, where the First Deputy Mayor of St. Petersburg Mr. A. Kudrin opened the workshop. Also the positive support of Mr. Z.A. Yakobashvili, Deputy Minister of Science and Technology Policy of the Russian Federation, S.A.Tsiplayev, Representative of the President of the Russian Federation in St. Petersburg and Mr. J.Glybin, Deputy Chairman of the State Committee of the Russian Federation for the Defence Industry were deeply appreciated by participants.

This is a book presenting a large number of articles from scientists and managers from NATO-countries and from Russia. The book also illustrates the workshop and roundtable discussions concentrated on inventory levels achieved in the past five years, the conversion of military enterprises and experiences and ideas on how to cope with the process in the future.

All scientists who participated in the workshop appreciated experiencing from some different countries and scope of the work and it is our hope that you as reader will also enjoy the content of this book.

Best wishes,

Wolfgang G. Puppe
General Manager
Head of Representative office
ABB Asea Brown Boveri
Artillerijskaya ul, 1,
191104 St. Petersburg, Russia

Dmitry V. Sergeev
First Vice-Governor
Chairman of the Committee
for Economics and Industrial Policy
16, Voznensky pr.
190000 St. Petersburg, Russia

Working Session I:
Conversion in a Changing World

ON SOME ASPECTS OF CONVERSION AT RUSSIAN ENTERPRISES

Yuriy A. GLYBIN
First Deputy Chairman
of the State Committee for Defence Industry
of the Russian Federation
Moscow

First and foremost, I would like to briefly touch upon the philosophy of the problem discussed here today. There is the item "Policy in Conversion" on the agenda of the seminar. The policy of the conversion process shall be established prior to the beginning of the process and shall determine the level, extent and terms of reduction in the development and production of weapons and military equipment. Within this process specialists and highly qualified personnel earlier engaged in manufacturing high-tech military products shall be transferred quite painlessly to the fabrication of products in demand on the market and the R&D potential shall be fully preserved.

The leader with which we competed and had parity in arms production and development – the United States of America, the leading country of NATO – reduces its military production not more than by 4–5 % a year. And we now have about 15–17 % of the military production we had in 1991. Therefore, at present it is too late to speak about the policy regarding the terms and ways of arms reduction. At present we have to speak about the methods and techniques necessary to fully preserve, first of all, the intellectual scientific and technological potential of our defence complex, as it shall serve and will serve Russia and its people. Russia is the only country which decided to carry out such a complicated and very expensive experiment where each rouble cut down in military expenses (while the number of people engaged in the army remains practically unchanged) entails 1.5–2 roubles of losses in industry. That is all to be said briefly on the philosophy of this item.

Conversion of defence industry in Russia makes an integral part of economic reforms carried out by the Government. The depth and general scale of the conversion processes taking place in Russia are unparalleled by their complexity, size and intensity in the world practice. Therefore, realising its responsibility for the results of the conversion, the State provides it with assistance and ensures, as far as feasible, financial support of enterprises.

The governmental program "Conversion of Defence Industry in 1993–1995" made the basis for the implementation of support provided by the state in this field. The objective of the program consisted in the following: to combine minimum reduction in the number of employees, maximum utilization of production and

W. G. Puppe et al. (eds.), Conversion of Military Enterprises, 3–6.

scientific-technological potential of the defence complex for civil applications and minimum expenses in defence industry reorientation and to obtain the maximum effect in the most important fields of the economic development. A task was set to preserve capacities of agricultural industry, heat and energy industry, ship-building, aviation, medicine, light industry and a number of other industrial branches.

In drawing-up the program the priority was applied to the conversion activities which implied : establishing of production to substitute imported products on the domestic market, orientation to the development and introduction of high-quality power– and resources-saving techniques and technologies, reorientation of production with the use of state-of-the-art technologies, new materials and products, increase in the development and production of dual-use equipment.

Production capacities established in 1992–1995 within the process of the said program implementation allowed manufacturing of civil products in demand on the domestic market, for instance diamond tools, liquid-crystal screens, equipment for fiber-optical communication lines, intensive-therapy breathing equipment and other medical equipment.

As a result of the above program implementation an international certificate was obtained for the plane "TU-204" of the Tupolev's firm. Certificates were got for helicopters "KA-32-1", "MI-34" and "MI-26" and a number of other kinds of such products. Volgograd plant of drilling equipment started the production of mobile setups of 80 t weight-carrying capacity for repairing and bringing oil and gas wells into production. On orders of the Russian Ministry of Public Health a number of plants started the production of medications, such as nitrosorbite, nitrogranulong and some others to substitute similar products imported.

At present the draft of a new program – "Governmental Program of Conversion in Defence Industry for 1995–1997" has been developed in compliance with the Decree of the Government. This new Program comprises a number of sub-programs – 8 in total, including those for aviation, ship-building, heat and power industry, medicine, electronics, communication, information science and new materials. The implementation of Program 1995–1997 will provide for continuous putting into operation of additional production capacities for manufacturing civil products for transport, communication and other branches of economy.

Ownership changes taking place in the defence complex now provide certain influence on success in conversion. More than 1,300 of former defence enterprises have been or are being reorganized into joint stock companies. However, the Russian defence nucleus shall be preserved in any case, as it determines manufacturing of the main military products both in R&D and in production. This nucleus consists of a little more than 400 enterprises which are not subject to privatization pursuant to the decision of the Government and shall remain federal property.

At present by the initiative of the President and the Government of Russia our Committee is preparing the federal program "National Technological Base". The main objective of the Program consists in the preservation and further development of the national technological base, i.e. the preservation of the intellectual potential of the Russian science. Certain attention is also paid to "dual-use" technologies. This Program implementation requires the settlement of a number of short-term and long-term tasks, first and foremost the following:

– preservation, modernization and development of the national technological base;

– technological re-equipment of industry;

– development of technologies ensuring increase in domestic products competitiveness;

– establishing scientific and technological base for future systems of various applications;

– training and qualification improvement of scientific and technological personnel;

– perfection of the system for governmental control over the technological development for the country;

– concentration of efforts by Russian researchers, scientists and manufacturers in the development, search and introduction, first of all, of general industrial technologies of key importance for the qualitative technological re-equipment and bringing products to the level of the best world samples.

The national technological base lays the foundation which will allow the achievement of priority purposes and solution of the most important tasks of the national Russian policy in science and intellectual production.

One of the tasks faced by conversion industry consists in their products introduction to the domestic and international markets. The main market instrument is certification as a procedure undertaken to confirm the products quality and stability in ensuring it within the whole cycle of design, manufacturing, supplies. To solve the problem of certification the Committee for Defence Industry jointly with a number of leading research institutes have established and registered the system of voluntary products certification and quality guarantee "Oboronsertifika". The main objective of this system consists in carrying out certification according to European and international standards and obtaining international acknowledgement of certificates issued under this system. "Oboronsertifika" is to contribute to the solution of an important governmental task of identification and providing support for competitive industrial technologies capable of ensuring fast recoupment of investments.

The personnel of defence enterprises – quality managers and experts-auditors are being trained and get practical experience. Standard base is being compiled for carrying out certification work proceeding from the necessity of harmonisation in Russian and international requirements to products. Working contacts have been set with the European Bank of Reconstruction and Development, with well known in the world firms "TUF" (Germany) and "Bureau Veritas" (England), as well as with other international institutions dealing in these activities.

Within the framework of the program "Conversion-Certification" implementation under the system "Oboronsertifika" regional certification centers are established jointly with regional administrations. That will allow the increase in the efficiency of conversion enterprises management, the reduction in expenses of certification systems establishing and achievement of products' high quality and competitiveness on the domestic and international markets.

Intellectual property problems have become of special importance under transition to market economy and entering the international division of labour. Without corresponding protection of R&D's and products it is very difficult to gain success even on the domestic market, to say nothing about the international one.

By the Decree of the Government the State Committee for Defence Industry has been authorized to undertake necessary steps to ensure the legal protection of intellectual property objects created at defence enterprises and to protect governmental, military and commercial interests. The State Committee for Defence Industry has developed the concept for distribution of rights to R&D results obtained due to state budget funding. The concept is intended to ensure the balance between the interests of enterprises, governmental customers, and the interest of employees (authors) in development and introduction of scientific and technological achievements.

The State Committee for Defence Industry of Russia has distinguished the leading institutions in industrial property aspects: Academy of Ship-Building – in transfer of scientific and technological achievements from defence to civil production; Research-Center "Informtekhnika" – in patent and licensing work. The makeup of the methodological council of the Committee for Patent-Licensing and Rationalization Work has been agreed upon. Annual seminars of patent-licensing agencies are arranged and the interest to them is constantly growing. Methodical recommendations have been developed for rationalization work, for defining profit and calculation of royalties for the use of inventions and industrial designs under the Patent Law of the Russian Federation.

The following methodical recommendations have been developed and are under approbation now: methodical recommendations for estimating the value of trademarks as industrial property objects; methodical recommendations for the payment of royalties for inventions used abroad and remuneration for assistance in patent protection of these inventions usage; methods for registration of intellectual property objects as intangible assets in privatization and reorganization of defence enterprises into joint-stock companies.

This work is mainly aimed at achieving the required quality standards and finding by enterprises their niches on the market. Unless we establish the institution and system for products certification and get our own "TUF" and "Bureau Veritas" we will hardly manage to enter the international market. That is proved by a number of examples given by mass media and the State Committee for Statistics. It is enough to mention that today the main part of the Russian export is formed of raw materials: gas, oil, metals, etc. The volume of machine-building products export decreased by dozens of times as a result of CMEA disintegration and cessation of deliveries to other European countries. Therefore, certification and marketing of industrial products will provide us with an opportunity to enter the international community as an equal partner and to preserve the scientific potential of Russia.

DEFENSE CONVERSION IN RUSSIA: BACKGROUND AND STATUS

David BERNSTEIN
Center for International Security and Arms Control
Stanford University
320 Galvez Street
Stanford, California 94305-6165 USA

1. Introduction

It is very useful to have a conference like this in which we get perspectives on conversion from different countries and then try to focus on the specific issues in the CIS with the views of industry, government, and the research community.

One of the important benefits of having all of these perspectives is to see if we all have the same concept of what we mean by conversion. My guess is that we do not have a common understanding on an international level. I doubt that we even have a common understanding of what we mean by conversion in a given country, for example Russia.

I would like to start by noting a few contrasts between the problems of and the environment for conversion in the United States and Russia. Second, I will discuss some aspects of conversion in Russia in greater detail based upon our five years of research, which has been supported by the Carnegie Corporation of New York and the Eurasia Foundation. Finally, I would like to discuss various modes of conversion in Russia.

2. Contrast Between Conversion in the United States and Russia

I have chosen these two countries because, although they were the two countries whose economies were most affected by the arms race of the Cold War, their problems of conversion are very different. The following are a few key contrasts:

- The Soviet/Russian economy was highly over-industrialized, and a very large fraction of its industry was devoted to military production. The industrial and military-industrial segments of the U.S. economy were in reasonable balance with the overall economy, although many would argue that the military portion started getting out of proportion in the early to mid–1980s.

W. G. Puppe et al. (eds.), Conversion of Military Enterprises, 7–14.

- The magnitude of the procurement reductions, as a percentage of GNP, in the Soviet Union and later in Russia was about a factor of 5 greater than in the United States, and most of it occurred in about two years as opposed to a decade in the United States. Economic statistics for the Soviet defense budget can not be considered to be highly accurate. Similarly, some current economic statistics in Russia are unreliable because of unreported economic activity.
- The primary strength and volume of the research, technology, and manufacturing bases in the Soviet Union/Russia was in the military industrial enterprises, whereas in the United States it was overwhelmingly in the commercial sector. Therefore while both countries are seeking dual-use approaches to integrating the civilian and military technology and manufacturing bases, they are approaching this goal from exactly opposite directions.
- The United States had a strong, functioning market economy in which to adjust to the reduction in military production. The Soviet Union/Russia had a weak, inefficient command economy without market-oriented institutions. So conversion in the Soviet Union/Russia had to be addressed simultaneously with much broader economic reform.
- The most receptive markets for conversion products in the United States were in high-technology sectors, whereas in the Soviet Union/Russia there was greater demand for consumer goods.
- There has been a lack of reliable statistical and market data in the Soviet Union/Russia to guide enterprises in the selection of new products. Market data were abundant and accurate in the United States, and the market was relatively saturated and stable.
- Global markets for U.S. goods were almost completely unaffected by the end of the Cold War, but the breakup of COMECON, and later of the Soviet Union, interrupted many of the markets for Russian products. It also interrupted chains of inputs.

3. Background on Conversion in Russia

There are great uncertainties in statistical economic data in the FSU, but most of the key points about conversion can he made without highly accurate quantitative data. The Soviet economy showed serious signs of stress in the late 1980s, and the Gorbachev government identified the high levels of military expenditures as one of the key causes of the economy's weakness. While it is impossible to accurately quantify the level of defense expenditures because of the inconsistent and inadequate means of accounting, most estimates run above 20 % of GNP. This is about three to four times higher than the rate in the United States, and the ratio of equipment procurement is probably even higher.

Following Gorbachev's 1988 speech to the United Nations, he undertook to reduce military expenditures, including procurement, and to start to convert a substantial portion of the military industry to civilian production. The stated goal was to go from a ratio of military to civilian production of 60/40 to 40/60. The attempt involved the conversion of many enterprises in the military-industrial complex, without downsizing, restructuring, or eliminating any of the enterprises. This effort was within the command economy structure; was not a part of a sufficiently comprehensive economic reform program; and was (at least in hindsight) unrealistic, poorly planned, and inadequately financed.

The Soviet defense industry constituted almost all of the technology base of the country. Almost all civilian production involving electronics and other forms of technology was carried out by the defense industry, which accounts for the 40 % of the output of the military industry that was civilian goods. This is in sharp contrast to the United States, where civilian technology, especially in electronics and computers, leads military technology in volume, sophistication, and rate of development by a wide margin. There are a few defense-unique technologies in the United States such as nuclear submarine propulsion and stealth.

With the collapse of the Soviet Union, Russia inherited a disproportionately large fraction of the Soviet military industrial complex, and hence the conversion problem has been greater for Russia than for the other newly independent states, although it is also a significant issue in several of the others. The Russian government continued, and accelerated, the reduction in military procurement as the economy continued to decline rapidly. At the same time, Russia also instituted a variety of economic reform programs intended to introduce a market economy. Planners considered that defense conversion would take place within this market (or at least transitional) economy. This potentially helped in that a market environment would ultimately improve the chances of conversion, but it exacerbated the nearterm problems in that the infrastructure of the command economy, however inefficient it was, was no longer fully functional, and it had not been replaced by a fully functional market-oriented infrastructure although many of its components now exist.

Nonetheless the Russian government did institute some conversion programs (as well as other programs, such as privatization and price liberalization), which, although they caused problems early on, eventually assisted the overall conversion process. The Russian conversion programs were certainly better thought-out than the Soviet programs, but they were still quite unrealistic and inadequately funded. In particular they did not include any downsizing or hard budget constraints.

Foreign programs were also instituted by the United States, European countries, and the international financial institutions to provide both financial and technical assistance. These programs were also not adequately planned, not coordinated with each other, slow to be implemented, and inadequately funded. As a result of all of these factors, most of the conversion that has taken place has been done by the enterprises or by workers themselves.

In the absence of coherent, sufficiently funded government programs, or adequate foreign assistance, the major burden of conversion has fallen on the enterprises. The enterprises have had to undertake major restructuring programs because they had not been structured to function in a competitive market economy. This restructuring can be thought of as having four major components:

1. Relationship to owners

There are in many cases a new set of owners, and these owners may have an interest in distribution of any profits and in major strategic decisions, whereas the old owner (State) was more interested in production than profitability. Since the State was both owner and customer, it had a conflict of interest.

2. Relationship to employees

Decisions regarding the size of the labor force and the services to be provided to workers will have to be based more on considerations of economic efficiency than before.

3. Internal organization

The boundaries of the firm were different in the command economy than in a market economy. Certain functions previously performed by the State must now he internalized, and functions not previously existing, such as marketing and finance, must he created.

4. Relationships to other outside organizations

Many outside organizations, such as suppliers, distributors, hanks, and legal services, must be dealt with more on a market-economic basis than before.

4. Conditions for Enterprise Conversion

Several conditions shape the environment in which the enterprises must attempt conversion. Listing these conditions will help illustrate that the conversion problem in Russia differs dramatically from that in any other country, and will form a basis for assessing the progress that has been made. Some of the most important conditions are:

- The magnitude and suddenness of the problem was unprecedented.
- The breakup of the Soviet Union and COMECON resulted in disruption of distribution of finished products and in inputs.
- The composite profile of industry was unsuited to functioning in a market economy. Some firms were too highly vertically integrated, building things in-house that could more efficiently he produced by outside suppliers; others were too little integrated, with separation of design bureaus and production facilities; monopolistic suppliers that were state controlled in the past were too strong when they were freed from state control; there was essentially no new entrant sector or sector of small high-technology companies which, in the West, contribute to both innovation and growth of employment; and interrepublic suppliers were isolated by new political and economic boundaries and barriers.
- There was a lack of capital and capital markets (including institutional mechanisms for mergers/acquisitions, divestitures, and spin-offs).

- There was a lack of commercial and legal infrastructure in which to conduct commerce.
- Crime and corruption, aside from being immoral, is a big effective "tax" on business, and not much of this tax is being recirculated into the economy. The resultant desire to withhold financial information from the Mafia also leads to concealing information and avoidance of legal taxes even more than would otherwise be the case.
- The backgrounds and experience of industry and government personnel were not well suited to operation in a market economy, and there was no labor market of skilled and experienced market-oriented businesspeople.
- Government policies of taxation, customs duties, export limitations, etc. were not conducive to investment and growth.
- There was little mobility of labor either professionally or geographically.
- There was a lack of government military procurement planning so that industry could not make its plans based on anticipated procurements.
- There was a lack of protection from imports, which on a mid-term basis could have assisted new commercial ventures and emergent industries to get a toehold in the domestic market.
- There was a lack of established equilibrium economy and market survey data to assist enterprises in selecting new products and services. Many analysts have faulted the enterprises for converting on the basis of technology push as opposed to market pull. While there is some validity in this criticism, there was also a great lack of useful data on markets, products, and competitive production potential on which to plan new product strategies.
- There were frequent changes of political power and government policy.
- There was a lack of hard budget constraints, and subsidies were not distributed selectively on the basis of conversion potential and accomplishment.
- Macroeconomic stabilization was delayed long into the economic reform program, leading to an inflationary condition that deterred investment and complicated planning.
- Potential foreign investors and Russian investees did not have a clear understanding of each others' objectives and practices.
- The international community did not have consistent, adequately financed programs of international assistance.

5. Modes of Conversion in Russia

5.1. ACTIVE CONVERSION

These are forms of conversion based on activities initiated by the enterprises.

- Total enterprise conversion. The old understanding of conversion and the one sought through the planned economy was for complete enterprises to change their mix of military and civilian production. This was to be done while maintaining the basic structure and size of the enterprise.

This form of conversion rarely occurs for several reasons:

- Lack of capital to finance conversion.
- Lack of demand for products selected.
- Inability to produce chosen products competitively in terms of value and price.
- Lack of corporate infrastructure and planning to implement conversion.

- Downsizing (possibly with new product introduction). The concept of purposely downsizing an enterprise to achieve an economic balance between costs and revenue was initially a difficult one for a Russian manager, or owner, to accept. It is an essential element of strategy of a firm in a market economy. Furthermore, it is necessary to downsize in advance of sales declines in order to avoid losses. Downsizing can also involve dropping product lines (military or civilian) that are proving to be unprofitable even though product development and production lines have already been established. Refusal to downsize results in the use of valuable resources to cover excess payrolls and other nonessential costs rather than to implement conversion strategies. In an attempt to utilize full staff, many enterprises attempted to make a large number of new products aimed at a variety of markets rather than concentrating on a very small number of activities and having adequate resources to follow through.
- Decentralization. This involves identifying the most promising technologies and/or product lines and isolating them from the other activities of the enterprise. This strategy allows the isolated elements to try to restructure at an economically efficient level without bearing unnecessary centralized overhead.
- Spinning off. A form of decentralization involves spinning off promising components of an enterprise and selling some of its ownership for capital investment or other needed assets. weaker. However, combined with downsizing it may he the most profitable approach in the long run.
- A less complete form of decentralization than spinning off components is to isolate a component's cost structure and to take outside (frequently foreign) contracts for manufacture or research. This can allow the formation of a cooperative venture without a long-term commitment being made before the business's viability is tested. It can serve as a preliminary step that can he followed by the spinning off and/or formation of a joint venture.
- Expansion of production of existing civilian product lines. In principle this is the easiest form of conversion. It is essential, however, to ascertain that there is enough market demand to absorb the increased production, and, even though the products may have been successful in the past, it is essential to improve efficiency of production (reduce costs) and possibly improve quality in anticipation of new competition.
- Development and production of new products. If these can be based on core competencies and provided to current customers, this is a reasonably conservative mode of conversion. However, it must he realized that other enterprises may he

coming into the same markets and that competition will increase. There are literally dozens of enterprises planning to produce microwave ovens, for example.

- One form of selecting new products is to shift from hightechnology military products to low-technology consumer goods. Many enterprises are understandably unhappy doing this. Their counterparts in other countries feel much the same; however, the market for high-technology products at this stage of the Russian economy is not nearly as high as the capability to design and produce them. Insistence on high technology by too many enterprises will inevitably result in the failure of many of them.

5.2. PASSIVE CONVERSION

These are forms of conversion that are not initiated by the enterprise, and in some cases may he actually opposed by it.

- "Brain drain." Many skilled people are leaving the defense enterprises on their own initiative to take other jobs. These other jobs include going into the commercial services sector, such as hanks; starting new companies; or even becoming cab drivers. From the standpoint of the enterprises, this is a loss of capability, but from a macroeconomic perspective, the industrial sector was bound to shrink. The enterprises that may be the most successful in retaining their top talent are those that were willing to downsize and reduce their excess labor so that they could better support their top talent both intellectually and financially.
- Moonlighting and sunlighting. There are people who are still technically on an enterprise's payroll but do not have work assigned. Some use the enterprise's facilities to conduct their own private businesses. Here again this is not necessarily to the advantage of the enterprise, but it does create economic activity. To the extent that the enterprises can encourage this intrapreneurship in exchange for participating in these new businesses, everyone can gain. This process can be formalized and encouraged by setting up new business incubators on the enterprise's premises.

5.3. DEFINITION OF CONVERSION IN RUSSIA

While it is very risky to rely on the statistical data, because of the magnitude of the gray (unreported) economic activity, the Russian economy seems to be flattening out. It may he too soon to say whether this is the bottom or just a pause in the decline. If the macroeconomic stabilization program continues to show progress, and if reforms continue, this may very well be the bottom.

In reaching this point, there have been dramatic declines in both military and civilian production, but the profile of the economy has definitely changed. Most military production enterprises have experienced dramatic declines in employment as well as in production. The service sector has grown, and the gray economy, which is nonmilitary, has also grown. There are more small businesses than before. Therefore the profile and not just the size of the economy has changed considerably. Although there are not many cases of complete conversion of defense enterprises, many of the assets of the military research and production infrastructure have shifted to be utilized for nonmilitary activities. These assets appear to be primarily human and technological, and secondarily physical and financial. These changes in the profile of the economy, with a reduction in the military component, is the most appropriate definition of conversion in RUSSIA.

There has obviously been some measure of success in this conversion process. It is difficult to say if it has been more or less than could be expected, since there is no historical precedent. Russia will not succeed on an American model or a European, Korean, or Chinese one. Russia will continue to develop the Russian model. In hindsight one can see many ways in which it could have been made more successful, but whether this is compatible with the overall economic and political reforms proceeding simultaneously is also difficult to say.

FRENCH EXPERIENCE WITH MILITARY CONVERSION

Emile BLANC
FRANCE CONVERSIA
32 rue de Lisbonne
75008 PARIS

I am delighted to have been given this opportunity to present a few examples of French experience with defence conversion in the context of the 'NATO Advanced Research Workshop" in St. Petersburg.

Let me first of all try to describe the situation of the French defence industry. That may help understand the phenomenon of conversion in my country and, in particular, identify some of its specific aspects. You may be able to extrapolate from the solutions adopted by us some elements that are applicable to other countries and to their defence sectors.

From 1980 to 1987 global defence outlays rose sharply (+60 %), and the defence industry throughout the world – with the sole exceptions of Germany and Japan – reflected this growth in terms of both sales and employees:

Direct employment:
1,000,000 in the USA
700,000 in Europe
of which 300,000 in France.

The years 1989–1993 saw a considerable contraction. The disappearance of threats brought about a substantial reduction of defence budgets, especially for military hardware, and a corresponding shrinkage of production in the industry. This was compounded by a drastic fall of exports. The Western countries and, more generally, all countries have progressively and more and more rapidly reduced their purchase of military hardware.

For a while France had fallen victim to an illusion: the ambitious goals of two program-laws – one aborted and one adopted – were no protection against the general pressure to reduce defence efforts.

Two indicators may help to illustrate this development:

– defence appropriations, continually reduced since 1990, should bottom out at 75 billion francs, a reduction of about 40 %

W. G. Puppe et al. (eds.), Conversion of Military Enterprises, 15–20.

– since 1985–1986 exports have fallen by almost 70 %, having passed through a period of decline, then temporarily stabilized, and once again fallen since 1990.

These changes have happened over a short time. They have already lead, or will lead, to drastic upheavals in the defence industry and in individual enterprises, with consequential technical, financial, social and human problems.

It is of little value to ask why the full magnitude of this problem has not been exposed, and none of the involved parties can today afford to dodge it and hope that defence allocations will return to anywhere near the levels of yesteryear. Everything, in effect, conspires to make restructuring inescapable. In addition to shrinking budgets, numerous other developments are at work and have amplified the problem: the exponential growth of R&D expenses, the globalization of the economy, internationalisation through dual use technologies, simultaneous engineering, the fractionated enterprise.

Some firms have anticipated these developments and, in one way or another, prepared for the contraction. Others have adopted a policy of "wait and see" and today find themselves in a critical situation.

I am not speaking about the latter category. Rather, I shall focus on an example I know well, namely the SNPE.

For five years I have been the president of this firm. I was engaged to continue some conversion activities and to start others. I want to share with you the lessons of that experience.

The state owns a large majority of the shares of the Societe Nationals des Poudres et Explosifs.

Contrary to some public belief, a state-owned enterprise (in this case SNPE) enjoys no special privileges. We are a normal limited liability company, a commercial enterprise with the state as the majority shareholder.

SNPE's Board of Directors includes representatives of a private bank, Societe Generale, of the employees, of the shareholder, and individuals with relevant qualifications who were appointed for their expertise.

SNPE has been a limited liability company since 1971, having previously been a public service ("Service d'Etat"). Its origins go back to 1336. Today it is at the apex of a group employing 5,600 people, with annual sales of 4.3 billion and net profits of 140 million francs, or 3.3 % of sales. The company specializes in weapons-related chemical products, and it develops and manufactures a range of civilian and military energy products, powder, explosives and propellants:

- Its main mission is to ensure the propulsion of the strategic missiles of our deterrent force and to supply the armed forces with powder, explosives and propellants.
- It is constrained to draw maximum benefit from its considerable R&D effort (16 % of turnover), both for the nation and for the company itself and, in particular, to investigate all possible applications in the fields of its core business.

In anticipation of the foreseeable difficulties in the military sector, this company, very early-on, began to seek complementary markets in related industrial sectors. It decided a long time ago to diversify and internationalize. Today, 2/3 of sales go to the civilian sector; of this, a considerable share is sold in free and highly competitive markets, for example pharmaceutical, health care and phyto-sanitary products, paints, nail polish, composites, hunt products and industrial explosives, etc..... As you can see, SNPE enjoys a fairly unique position and exemplifies the defence contractor of the future, semi-civilian and semi-military. It is worth pointing out that, with the exception of DCN and GIAT INDUSTRIES, French defence contractors make on average more than 2/3 of their sales to the civilian sector. This unusual situation – for the largest American defence contractors the corresponding figure is less than one-third – proves that they have made the cuts in successive French defence budgets the starting point for their implementation of a policy of restructuring through conversion.

I should emphasize the particularities of the military compared with the civilian market, because, in effect, the term conversion has come to signify the transition from a military to a civilian activity.

We must remember that a defence contractor has as its customers defence ministries, in the first instance that of its own country, i.e., a single and powerful public-sector client.

The public sector customer knows its requirements perfectly well and knows how to express them, in the form of precise specifications in terms of technical features and maintenance in an operational state, both for complex systems and for individual items. The defence contractor has thus relatively little influence on the identification and the expression of the customer's requirements. Advertising will not influence the customer's decision, it will not even affect it. On the other hand, the customer is much better informed than is the case in other markets. The defence contractor is much more shaped by the market than it can define or direct it. This is a fundamental difference between civilian and military customers, but it is not the only one. Generally speaking, the military customer has requirements, resources, budgetary resources even, that are determined in advance, solid and stable – or at least it is credited with these attributes.

As a rule, the military customer has clear guidelines for approving its orders and purchases, and it is prudent to observe these norms strictly. Often it also has special requirements, perfectly justified, over and above the stated requirements. For all these reasons the defence contractor's relations with the customer can never be the same as those with customers in free civilian markets.

It is not really a problem to adapt to the civilian market, but its is nonetheless a prerequisite for success to be aware of the differences. I shall borrow Murray Weidenbaum's list of essential differences. We at SNPE have been acutely conscious of them. All our employees at every stage of production, marketing and after-sales service are fully familiar with the concepts of competitiveness, risk-taking, and total client satisfaction.

Defence conversion is a complex task that requires time, money and ideas, as well as........a bit of luck.

Our efforts have led to the formulation and application by SNPE of a few rules:

Defence conversion is not marely the substitution of civilian for military products. It is important to look for products the manufacture of which calls for the same or related technologies and is, or can be, carried out with the existing plant and equipment. The main intention behind this rule is to reduce to a minimum the need for new investment – material as well as immaterial.

Our first derivative products naturally were first and foremost energy products. SNPE has turned to:

- solid-fuel civilian space propulsion (REGULUS)
- direct derivatives of nitrocellulose: paints, varnishes, bases for nail polish (BERGERAC, ITALNITRO, TEVCO [US])
- civilian explosives (NOBEL EXPLOSIFS and its affiliates)
- automotive safety and air bags. LIVBAG uses SNPE's solid propellant to inflate the bags.

However, our efforts have also included related technologies and techniques. The basic constituents of high-performance composites, i.e., resins and pre-impregnants, as well as the development of components and their production in small or large series: STRUCTIL, BRUNET, SICAP, MELCO. Our work in this field is far from completed. STRUCTIL is successfully pursuing development efforts aimed at obtaining the approval of space contractors for its resins and pre-impregnants and thereby opening up a new high-technology market.

Diversification from military chemicals based on nitration, phosgenation and hydrogenation technology, which is highly developed at SNPE, aims at developing intermediary products with multiple applications, active agro-chemicals (FRAMOCHEM – Hungarian – and SISSA – French-Japanese). This is one of the pillars of conversion at SNPE. This activity has led to the successful penetration of the North American and Asian markets and shows good prospects for the markets offerd by PECOS and the UKRAINE.

Five companies are active in the pharmaceutical sector: ISOCHEM and its subsidiaries apply the major pharmaceutical technologies: organic synthesis, peptide synthesis, vegetable extraction. This is one of the most beautiful blossoms of the SNPE group.

All of these diversification and conversion activites were either developed internally – true conversion – or in partnership with other firms, or by way of acquisition, so as to achieve as quickly as possible a significant position in the target market or market niche. Each of these three methods has its own advantages. Their application in a particular case is a matter of opportunity and efficiency. In its essence, the process is Darwinist. Not every effort succeeds. We have suffered our defeats and set-backs: radio-reticulable resins, isocyanides, phosphoric solvents, thermostable polymers, industrial adhesives .... were abandoned. It is important to be wise enough to abandon an activity if there is no market for it.

What have been the main lessons?

Any new product must meet the requirements of a market that has been carefully defined and researched. It must be introduced through a responsive and highly commercial distribution chain. It should generally be a "connected product", i.e., one that is complementary to a product already in the market – such as nail polish and lipstick – or a component of a new complex product that is being launched with major publicity – e.g., the air bag.

As a general rule, success is assured if the product is well chosen and sufficient resources are provided.

The new product must have a unit cost lower than its transfer or selling price so as to leave a profit. This golden rule of the market economy for the product-market duo strongly applies to conversion. The activity must be profitable. For the firm this is a prerequisite for survival. It may be that losses are incurred in the start-up phase, but that condition must not allowed to become permanent. You have got to have the courage to stop once you become conscious of the situation. How much conversion activity has failed, and with it how many enterprises, because it was not diagnosed in time as destined to fail.

Besides the product-market and the strictly economic aspects, conversion raises other issues:

The social aspect must not be overlooked. All conversion activity involves more or less complementary training of the workforce. Each of its members must find his or her place and be integrated in the new manufacturing, selling or product-support process.

Often problems with conversion arise as a result of a crisis and excess capacity. Surplus employees must be reassigned to acceptable positions. A whole range of measures must be designed to shed surplus personnel amicably, especially by offering them alternative employment. SNPE had a peak workforce of 8,000 (7,000 in the mother company). Today the workforce of the subsidiaries has risen from 1,000 to 3,000, that of the mother company fallen from 7,000 to also 3,000. In 10 years there has ben a net personnel reduction of 2,000, or 200 per year, mostly by natural attrition. No jobs have been lost through forced personnel reduction, but all jobs have profoundly changed. The absorption came primarily from transfers to newly established subsidiaries and new jobs created on site or in near-by locations. A specialized entity, SNPE CONVERSION, was established to attract new activities to existing SNPE plants.

Problems of salary and wage adjustment can also arise: civilian production can rarely support salary levels customary in the defence industry. Humane solutions must be developed that involve training, job reclassification and improved career prospects.

Considerations of regional policy must not be overlooked. For historic reasons our defence industry is located far from our eastern frontier. Where it is located today – in agricultural regions – it has become an important economic factor.

Solutions must be found that satisfy the local authorities. With their help SNPE has developed solutions: conversion products in the fields of energy products, barbecue lighters, fire lighters.

All of these measures have ensured that no-one or almost no-one has "fallen by the wayside". Each employee has had the possibility of being re-integrated or to find an individual solution through professional requalification. Social plans have been implemented successfully. This has taken time, it has imposed considerable financial charges on the company, which it has borne well since, with the appointment of a new president, the company has returned to excellent profitability.

I have already mentioned that conversion calls for the mobilisation of financial resources. The amounts often exceed the means of the enterprise, and it must be pointed out that the external assistance made available to-date has fallen short of even the minimum requirements. I consider this highly regrettable, because the problems only grow with the passage of time.

In any event, investments must be realised as soon as possible after the market opportunities have been identified. As a rule, to wait means to cede one's place to a competitor and thus to miss an opportunity.

SNPE has adapted its organigram to the new allocation of activities. Three major product groups have been identified. The number of our subsidiaries may appear excessive, but I have accepted that, as a rule, all energy should be focused in a specialized entity on a given market and on the products it can absorb.

Civilian production dominates and accounts today for some 2/3 of turnover. Ten years ago it accounted for 1/3. Its weight will increase further, but this does not mean that our basic mission will suffer.

The case of SNPE is not unique, but it may serve as an example of the results that can be achieved when a strong determination not to go under becomes the basis for activities aimed at adapting in order to survive.

I could have described numerous other examples:

- THOMPSON, especially its BRIVE factory, which used to sell 70 % of its output to the military sector and today aims to achieve a share of 80 % of total sales in the market for civilian electronics, the result of a complete restructuring of its production methods.
- DASSAULT Electronique with its subsidiary Dasault Automatismes et Telecommunicatiuons (DAP), which has shown some success: portable payment terminals, pocket phones. It operates in a difficult market. The firm does not give up, especially in view of its high level of technological know how.
- DASSAULT AVIATION with its civilian aircraft (model CORPORATE) and the success of its latest models.
- SAGEM. This company was a specialized defence contractor but has over time developed related civilian markets and today realizes more than 50 % of its turnover in civilian telecommunications and only 20 % in the defence sector.

All of these firms are members of FRANCE CONVERSIA. If you wish, our association can put you in touch with one or the other of its members that may be of interest to you.

THE POLICY OF EBRD TOWARDS MILITARY CONVERSION

Thierry MALLERET
EBRD, United Kingdom

This paper has no other ambition than describing the principles that determine the way in which the European Bank operates in the area of defence conversion. As you may know, the EBRD has been created to support the transition process to the market economy. Therefore, every single transaction concluded by the Bank, whatever the sector may be, is ultimately aimed at developing the private economic activity. Defence conversion is no exception to that rule, although we observe that the defence industry constitutes an unusual case because it represents one of the few sectors where the state endeavours to maintain governance for reasons of national sovereignty. In Russia, as in many Western countries which possess a strong defence base, this type of industry is still in the grip of national politics.

How do we tackle the conversion issue? I will first highlight the reasons for which EBRD supports it and some very simple ideas which illustrate why – in our view – the process is eventually worthwhile. Conversion projects match EBRD's mandate: in this area the Bank is highly additional since most Western investors would be unwilling to proceed without the guarantees and the risk mitigations it provides. In addition, conversion projects have a positive transition impact since they support the opening up of the Russian defence sector to commercial interests. Why does it make sense from an economic point of view to support it? We believe that investing in dual-use technologies the case for most defence enterprises – represents a risky choice since this sector is particularly vulnerable to the intensity of the world competition and the rapidly evolving technologies. However, Russia does possess a competitive advantage which is primarily based on the combination of a very skilled workforce and low labour costs (about 80–90 per cent below EU average). This competitive advantage compensates for the relatively low productivity levels (about one third below Western standards) and demonstrates that continuing improvement in productivity will be essential to ensure that competitive positions are maintained.

Although it appears difficult to anticipate the effects of the likely exchange rate appreciation anticipated in Russia over the short and medium term on export potential and import substitution, one might assume that import-substitution benefits of diversification will remain strong.

To put it in a nutshell, in the long run, we feel that the conversion from defence to civilian production should attract many strategic foreign investors because the

W. G. Puppe et al. (eds.), Conversion of Military Enterprises, 21–24.

absorption capacity of the internal market is huge, while the cost of entry remains very low.

I would like also to make a methodological remark and point out that we use the word conversion, but what we really mean is diversification. Conversion per se is extremely difficult to realise and examples abound all around the world of conversion failures. By contrast, diversification allows expansion of the civilian core business in a military enterprise which may devote only 10–20 % of its total production to the military activity. This is the case today in Russia.

There is no need to expand on the titanic difficulties the conversion process is currently facing in the Former Soviet Union. I will just mention that too large an expectation regarding the role of international institutions ought to be disregarded. By analogy with Beckett's famous play "Waiting for Godot", we could observe that Russian industry should not wait for Godot. Godot will not come because he does not exist. The conversion needs in the Bank's 25 countries of operation are so considerable that the resources of one or even several institutions would not be sufficient to meet them. In Russia, for example, the cost of converting or diversifying the defence industry is estimated at ranging from USD 150 to 200 billion. Even if the European Bank were to devote all its resources to foster the conversion process in the Former Soviet Union only, this would represent in the end an infinitesimal contribution (to make a comparison, President Clinton decided to allocate in the next few years US$ 20 billion – twice the capital of the EBRD – for conversion in the United States).

Therefore, the most sensible way to proceed is to create a critical mass of replicable conversion cases. In other words, the aim is to register a few "success stories" which could then exercise a snow-ball effect on the conversion process itself, with a spin-off effect on the business environment. In that respect, attracting and gaining the support of foreign joint venture partners constitutes the cornerstone of the Bank's conversion policy. In effect, joint ventures offer many advantages: they enable us to carve out a fraction of the production facilities which can then be privatised; they provide the expertise and the know-how, they train the local management along Western lines and improve managerial methods; they establish in the local economy some development poles; they help in demonopolizing the economy; and finally, they accelerate the transition process.

Obviously, domestic investment opportunities for conversion abound, but most of them are beyond the current means of the Bank because of its commitment to sound banking principles and the constraints on its equity investment portfolio. By and large, debt instruments cannot be utilised because of the financial situation of most enterprises and governance issues.

Principles approved by the Board require the Bank to equity invest only when it.

- perceives clear potential exit strategies;
- projects an internal rate of return commensurate to the risk.

You may notice that immediate privatisation does not constitute an absolute prerequisite. Obviously, the Bank favours those projects which offer a clear prospect of privatisation, but will not systematically exclude state-owned companies. In the field of defence conversion, one cannot afford to be too demanding because bankable opportunities are very limited indeed. Therefore, conditions which should be met before a project is seriously considered derive from common sense rather than "religious dogma". However, defence enterprises in the former Soviet Union do not - or very rarely – meet these criteria since many of them are currently in danger of further deterioration and collapse. In fact, very few of them are yet in a position to borrow money on commercial terms from an international bank. Why? To put it in a nutshell, any bankable project encounters the following general problems (setting aside the economic and political difficulties); uncertain legal framework, no audited financial statements, liquidity crisis, uncertainty about ownership rights, and lack of knowledge in preparing business proposals. Furthermore, and this is particularly relevant to the defence industry, the transformation of these big conglomerates into stock companies and their subsidiaries into companies with limited liabilities sometimes proves to be a nightmare, exactly as it was in East Germany when the Treuhand found that for most companies, total liabilities exceeded the realisable value of their assets. These "kombinates" would be due for liquidation if normal economic rules were applied. However, some of them possess a strong potential for surviving and prospering if they are given the proper assistance (both financial and technical). Therefore, EBRD concentrates on:

- providing technical assistance to pave the way for investment;
- stabilising enterprises currently in a critical condition, but potentially viable, so that they might be able to operate profitably in a market economy;
- attracting, and sharing the financial risk with local and foreign corporate investors who would otherwise have scaled down or cancelled their investment plans.

To transpose the famous formula from Ken Adelman and Norm Augustine in their article published by Foreign Affairs in December 1991, one might say that EBRD record of defence conversion is one unblemished by success. For the time being, the European Bank has slightly less than 20 conversion projects, in the pipeline. The majority of these are at an exploratory stage while a few are more advanced. They cover several countries (with a strong emphasis on Russia) and a wide range of industrial products from satellite launching rockets and integrated circuits to refitting of railway cars, forklifts and furniture production. Twenty is simultaneously very few and quite many. Very few in the light of what needs to be done, but many when one considers the constraints faced when tackling conversion. To give an order of magnitude, at the end of July 1995, about 80 joint-ventures were directly involved in conversion and diversification in Russia, representing about USD 800 million in investment. Western partners mix some huge blue-chips companies and small high-tech firms or even start-ups. However, the role played by the European Bank cannot be measured in terms of figures alone, As a direct result of its policy to stabilise, restructure and privatise certain companies, the Bank, in reality, is making a contribution to a positive and irreversible transformation of these economies. We understand that we are just putting a drop in the ocean, but this may be a drop of ink which might colour the sea. Should you have any questions, I would be happy to expand on a few projects already launched by the Sank in some very large enterprises such as Lomo or Perm motors or entire sectors such as the Air-Traffic Control.

Before concluding, I would like to make a final remark. The main problems associated with the state governance of enterprises are well known: ex-ante control (leading to meddling) rather than ex-post (that is to say, judging results), multiple objectives (i.e. non-commercial objectives such as employment combined with profit maximisation), multiple principals, and lack of competition. However, privatisation works efficiently only when it modifies the behaviour of the firm, which depends to a certain extent on the role of the state and its articulation with free initiative. Clearly, the creation of a proper entrepreneurial climate relies upon the promotion of entrepreneurs, in other words upon the creation of a situation where individuals shoulder their own responsibilities. In this respect, the state has a number of crucial responsibilities, since there are many areas such as the creation of a legal framework, a viable and fair taxation system, an effective competition policy, a decent social security system, an efficient education system, the acceptance of public order, etc. where it has a fundamental role to play. To put it very simply, the market and democracy will only thrive where and when the state has the means to protect them.

Working Session II:
Structural Conversion of Industry

STRUCTURAL ASPECTS OF DEFENCE CONVERSION IN THE RUSSIAN FEDERATION

Dmitriy V. SERGEEV
Chairman
Industrial Enterprises Association, St. Petersburg

Conversion and structural aspects of the Russian economy

As evidenced by Russia's many-years experience in defence conversion, the conversion processes have been carried out inconsistently and at times spontaneously. Having formally been responsible for conversion for more than 5 years, the Military-Industrial Complex (MIC) has arrived nowadays at the dangerous point, namely, the complete decay of science, production and manpower. Aggravation of the intersectoral disbalance (including non-payments), redoubling of inter-regional disproportion, worsening of the climate for international activities, etc. can hardly leave one optimistic about the future of the Russian conversion.

Let us consider the question: how much objective is the lamentable situation with conversion in our days and what are the ways out?

The basic feature of the conversion process in Russia is its time coincidence and close relationship with a most severe structural crisis of the home economy. In general, this relationship can be characteriÿed by two factors. First, the Russian economy seems exhausted to start growing again. This makes inevitable the drastic disbalance we observe in the present economic structure and, consequently, the impossibility to maintain the former levels of financing of defence enterprises, which, in its turn, has logically resulted in the necessity of conversion. Second, the difficulties inherent to the Russian conversion have aggravated the economic crisis in Russia and hindered the state to conduct any sensible policy, including industrial.

With regard to said above, one can make the following conclusion: the Russian conversion has a structural character and cannot be considered separately from the crisis-related changes characteristic of any transition economy. This is one of its main differences from the conversion process in advanced Western countries.

Having a structural character, the Russian conversion is a contradictory process. We distinguish the following contradictions:

1. The today priority production sectors (Agro-Industrial Complex, Fuel Energy Complex) directed at the satisfaction of consumer's demands, require comparatively simple technologies which do not need the high-tech equipment the defence industry is used to have produced. So, the problem is how to turn from the excessively high level

W. G. Puppe et al. (eds.), Conversion of Military Enterprises, 27–31.

of technologies to a much lower level if there are neither technical nor production possibilities to do it.

2. To overcome the structural crisis, defence enterprises have to master new kinds of production, get used to a new nomenclature, production scale, structure and level of production costs, put up with the long duration of the production innovation process, etc. How can one meet new requirements if one's scientific, production and manforce resources formed over a period of many decades are directed at a very narrow range of problems, are inflexible and hardly usable for other purposes.

3. A most severe structural crisis of the home economy has led to such a situation when one has practically neither time nor resources to carry out conversion. Moreover it hinders the evolution of conversion processes, which adds to the general problem of the compensatory weapon trade on the world market. All this brings us to the following question: how can we carry out defence conversion by some evolutionary way, rather than a revolutionary way inevitable nowadays when the resources needed for this purpose are strictly limited.

Therefore, the structural character of the Russian conversion lies in the disparity between the level of the scientific, production and manforce potential of defence enterprises and the limited resources and dates the conversion is forced into.

So the task of the defence industry is to realize restructuring within unrealistic terms and at unrealistic levels without having resources enough for this purpose. However, one should honestly admit that such a situation is quite objective and is predetermined by the deepening crisis which is far more ahead of the rearrangement potential of the home economy.

Conversion needs clear guidelines as to what is of priority in the economic structure

Conversion contradictions caused by the structural crisis are to be taken into account in developing the concept of conversion in Russia. We cannot still identify the main features and realise to a full extent what drastic consequences the crisis of the Russian economy may have. The sad example is some present approaches towards the management of the conversion process. Unfortunately, conversion programs and projects developed nowadays are still based on such parameters as if the Russian economy is stable or goes up.

The inadequate estimate of the dynamics of structural changes predetermined the major drawback of the conversion policy, which is the disparity between the limited resources and the desire to maintain all kinds of activities at once (and what makes it worse, at the same or even growing technical and production levels). Naturally, this sharpens the problem of the constant lack of financing, while the number of conversion programs and projects is abundant. As a result, we have achieved nothing.

The conversion in Russia is of crisis nature. Therefore one cannot expect the conversion in Russia to be successfully realized in civilized, state-controlled conditions as planned by the existing conversion programs. One should not have any illusions in respect of a possible combination of conversion with the overall economic changes (price liberalization, privatization, demonopolization, etc.) in the Russian Federation.

The structure of our economy being so deformed, the announced reform is only a mirror of a frightful economic disorder and appears to be another proof of the inability of the state to manage the economic processes. In conversion, for example, it resulted in a failure of any attempts to control conversion processes at the state level.

To stabilize the situation in conversion, one needs to take anti-crisis measures both at the state level and at the level of each enterprise subject to conversion. In the first case it is necessary to substantially correct the economic policy and strengthen the state control over economy. The main objective of the economic policy must be stopping of the decline observed in priority spheres, i.e. production of consumer's goods, rather than achievement of some financial balance in macroeconomy by any means. The anti-crisis measures must cover all levels of state control, including the regional one. This point is of the most immediate relation with conversion.

While developing the concepts of conversion, one should closely consider the tendencies (dynamics) of economic changes. And they are rather unfavorable. Therefore, a certain step-by-step approach is to be assumed. One should start with the anti-crisis model of conversion providing for respective anti-crisis measures. Then, after the priority spheres have been stabilized, it will be possible to pursue the immediate tasks of restoration and development of conversion enterprises, including their restructuring and renovation.

However the state is able just to determine the anti-crisis priorities. In reality, only the establishment of new economic relationships can form the basis for overcoming of the economic crisis. This, in its turn, makes conversion enterprises rearrange their production to meet requirements they are not used to, but which correspond to the crisis conditions. It is important to master the production oriented at the objectively decreasing buying capacity of consumers. Having a great respect for the attempts of enterprises to master new products, one should honestly recognize: either these products are old-fashioned, hardly modified, or they are new (in some cases high-tech), but not meeting the anti-crisis requirements.

Therefore, the main constructive proposal for the present moment is to combine the state anti-crisis economic policy with anti-crisis reorganization. In this respect, the measures taken by the state and enterprises are to be co-ordinated, since unilateral measures, as evidenced by life, are usually a failure.

An important form of co-ordination of state economic policy priorities with the respective activities at enterprises is the anti-crisis management combined with the use of investments or other kinds of support for priority projects and industries. This will create the basis for the reduction of non-priority industries and the gradual reorientation of resources at the needs of priority spheres, which will result in their further expansion. Only after that, the evolution of the domestic goods market will be possible, while the role of the state will be diminished. The concept development and the beginning of realization of the above tasks will create rich soil for separate, constructive proposals, and not vice versa.

At present we witness the abundance of separate, local, proposals (concerning e.g. non-payments, taxation, financial-industrial groups etc.) which cannot be brought into life or appear to be of low efficiency because of the lack of any sensible anti-crisis mechanism for their realisation. The development and introduction of such a mechanism would endow these proposals with more reality, whereas now they turn into just another futile campaign.

Anti-crisis thinking in order to overcome the conversion crisis

In the conditions of the protracted economic crisis, the anti-crisis thinking and methods of management are to be the main sources of impact on conversion processes. Experts from the Association of Industrial Enterprises of St. Petersburg have studied specific behavior models for conversion enterprises in crisis conditions and identified certain behavior patterns and their possible impacts on conversion.

A part of obtained results is included in the Informational Report on Conversion Problems which has been distributed among the participants of the seminar.

In general, the analysis of the conversion activity pattern in crisis conditions performed by the Association brings us to the following conclusions:

- the present crisis objectively (independently of the will of the heads of enterprises) leads to the use of anti-crisis methods of management;
- the anti-crisis activities of an enterprise are often just the opposite to what can be effective in the conditions of economic growth or stabilization;
- in industry an anti-crisis model of conversion activities is being formed spontaneously; it should be studied, fully recognized and used.

One should mention that different managers' reaction to the crisis tendencies is different, both from the time and perceptional standpoints. Both the domestic and world experience shows that, as a rule, people get aware of a crisis situation with a delay, which naturally leads to certain negative consequences. Formation of a false stereotype of the financial stability and economic growth prevents the survival of the military complex. Instead of anti-crisis measures, military enterprises appear to be more busy with innovation projects which are hardly appropriate for the crisis conditions. In the optimal case, such an activity will result in a mere imitation of the new conditions, but in the worst, it may lead to a further development of destructive processes.

The factors below seem to hinder the anti-crisis line of behavior:

1) The informational systems and methods of work with information at conversion enterprises turn out to be of little help for identification and prediction of crisis tendencies, for they are initially oriented at stable "external" (in relation to enterprises) conditions.

2) The delay may become even longer due to the psychology of the military complex administration who are rather inclined to follow their previous, familiar line and reject the new, "crisis", information contradicting their past experience until it is too

late. And the more success an enterprise was in the past, the more probable it is that its administration will psychologically reject any new information of a crisis character.

3) The delay may be aggravated by the possible menace to the status of an enterprise or its head, since the presently carried out anti-crisis activities may cast some doubt on the importance of this or that enterprise subject to conversion.

Plus to the above-mentioned factors, the conversion process becomes even more complicated because of the management crisis, which means the following:

- problems arise all of a sudden, against all expectations and available experience;
- the models and methods of management used to be efficient in the conditions of economic stability or growth turn out unacceptable during the crisis.

In essence, the main reason for the management crisis in the process of conversion is related with the fact that the existing structure of production, economic relations and resources does not meet the requirements of the crisis period.

Therefore, the absence of any basis for market economy in Russia, the long stability period in the past and severity of the present structural crisis result in the non-standard reaction of conversion enterprises toward the necessity of structural changes. The new, crisis, reality is absolutely different from the conditions the enterprises are used to. The conversion methods used during the stable period are hardly acceptable during the crisis, which is worsened by the lack of stable economic relations and the decline of the priority spheres of production. Any attempts to use these methods will only aggravate the whole situation.

Of course, one cannot become aware of the urgent need to revise the existing conversion methods and adjust them for the use in the crisis conditions in one instant. The question is whether the participants of the conversion process are ready to revise the strategy of conversion activities, work out a new, anti-crisis, strategy in order to survive, change into a new management system. It is important to realise the objective nature of the crisis tendencies inevitable at this very stage of the Russian economy.

A better understanding of the current events and their dynamics in the nearest future will be of great value for the development of the relevant anti-crisis model of conversion. For this purpose the anti-crisis thinking is needed. The elucidation of some features and patterns of such a thinking was the main objective of the present report.

PROJECT EXPERIENCE IN RUSSIA – A CONSULTANTS VIEW

Wolfgang G. PUPPE
DOWC Ost-West-Consult
Dresdner Bank group
Director on East Europe

The exchange of experiences and ideas amongst this group is extremely important and will certainly be of considerable benefit to those responsible in the CIS, the Russian Federation and the people concerned from the NATO member states.

With your permission I would first like to say a little about our own activities, to make it clear to you where our experience comes from. DOWC Ost-West-Consult are management consultants and a fully-owned subsidiary of Dresdner Bank in Germany headquartered in Frankfurt/Main. Our company was set up in 1990 with the aim of counselling business firms and state institutions in the process of transition from a planned to a market economy. Meanwhile we have conducted several hundred projects in the New German States and practically all the countries in Central and Eastern Europe. We have been active in Russia since 1991. In collaboration with a Russian partner we launched a joint venture in St. Petersburg, and together we now advise mainly Western companies seeking business openings in Russia or wishing to establish production facilities and joint ventures. We also advise Russian companies on restructuring and help them look for Western partners. It is interesting that our Russian partner CDB Rubin, is also a company in the armaments industry; so our joint venture does itself make a small contribution toward conversion.

We also operate in Russia and the C.I.S. states as consultants on behalf of the European Union and various development banks such as the EBRD in London and the Reconstruction Loan Corporation in Frankfurt/Main. Back in 1992 Mr. Sobchak commissioned us to conduct an initial review of the armaments industry and hightech potential in St. Petersburg in the form of a database, which has been marketed worldwide.

But I do not intend continuing this list. The important thing is that all the project which we carry out repeatedly revolve around the following issues:

1. How can we position the Russian companies with a new strategic market alignment in view of their drastic slump in turnover?

2. How can we now secure maximum sales of marketable products in the Russian market, in the C.I.S. and also in other Western countries?

W. G. Puppe et al. (eds.), Conversion of Military Enterprises, 33–36.

3. How can we train the management in modem management methods and how can we introduce these right down to the factory floor? ISO 9000 quality standards are just one issue, but this illustrates what we must aspire to.

4. How can new cooperation between Western and Russian companies be built up and made efficient?

5. Who is going to finance the prospects emerging from such cooperation?

At the last question all eyes naturally turn to our parent company. Dresdner Bank committed itself to Russia very early on. It has been represented in Moscow since 1972. Together with the Banque Nationale de Paris, BNP, it opened the first strictly Western bank on Russian territory two years ago in St. Petersburg. This joint venture bank has also a branch in Moscow, and there are also representative offices in several other locations. Business ties with local banks have been close for some years.

We are repeatedly asked by Western businessmen and Russian managers why so many attempts fail and what the major obstacles to the establishment of cooperation are. My first response is always that most of the projects founder on a lack of knowledge of the other side. Expectations and assessment of the desired partner's intentions and possibilities are generally unrealistic. Most Russian managers interested in cooperation assume that their Western partners have almost unlimited financial resources at their disposal; and as well as opening up the Western market they are also expected to build up production with know-how and capital. The Russian side does not appreciate that although the West perceives Russia as a market with great potential it is ultimately only one of several markets. Investment will be made here only if the risks are calculable and the anticipated yields are at least as high as in other countries. Neither is the case in most of the proposals made by the Russian side. Above all, the Russians are not sufficiently familiar with markets or methods of assessing the profitability of investment.

Conversely, the Western side often finds it very hard to accept that the criteria on which Russian businessmen and executives base their decisions and their motivation are usually quite different from those in the West. Western partners frequently have difficulty in estimating what negotiating and assertive powers Russian managers really have and in seeing their way through the web of interests within which the Russians are obliged to operate.

The privatisation of many big companies, especially in the armaments industry, is not yet complete and the allocation of duties frequently vague. There is direct and indirect administrative intervention and great pressure in the workforce. All this restricts the room for manouevre.

The projects running under title Defense Conversion, are certainly most difficult with regard to their terms of reference:

1. Almost all the companies are giants in terms of their organisation and workforce. Hardly any of them employ fewer than 10,000 people.

2. Once-stable government contracts have been reduced to between 20 and 30 %.

3. Many military products are no longer saleable because there is no market for them. National and international restrictions are imposed on those military goods that are saleable.

4. The companies have highly qualified staff, who are supposed to continue carrying out high-level work and wish to do so. From an economic viewpoint their level of qualification rules out solutions leading from hightech to primitive products and technologies.

5. Over the decades secrecy in the armaments industry – an understandable policy – has created special behavioural patterns for its managers. These do no exactly facilitate the communication needed for effective and successful cooperation.

What have we achieved in our conversion and restructuring projects and what experience and suggestions do we have?

From the early days of Russian conversion right after Gorbatchevs demilitarization effort in 1988 until today, military conversion in Russia was characterized by its adherence to conversion in sensu strictu, that is, the utilization of existing defense plants and staff at the same factory site to produce non-military products. It is partially the fault of Western experts, preaching this strict form of military conversion as an ultimate goal for Russia, that the experience with conversion has led to disillusionment and anger.

Our research and our experience with conversion and restructuring projects tell us quite a different story: military conversion in its strict sense never worked, does not work and will not work. There simply is no market demand for conversion products and therefore the abandonment of military conversion is not only rational, its is as well the right approach.

Of course, the general principal behind conversion – to use military technology for peaceful causes and to make the world a safer place – is not to question. But conversion per se is not sufficient to reach that goal. We have got to find the right form of conversion to make sure that demilitarization takes place and that the converted resources survive this noble effort.

85 per cent of American conversion projects have ended with complete failure. The few examples of success could be found in new niche markets and in segments, where military and civilian technology were quite similar, that is dual use products. So my first message to you is: forget military conversion in its strict sense, unless your posses innovations or dual-use technology.

The more integrated your approach to demilitarization is, the more success you will have: a combination of cooperation, downsizing, specialization, diversification and takeovers has proved to promise more success than any disintegrated approach. This holds true for any country in question: the U.S.A., Russia, Germany, China and so forth. But if you take a look at this broad approach to conversion, we are not talking about conversion anymore, but about military restructuring, which is quite similar to restructuring of any other – civilian or military – plant in the world. So my second advice is: use an integrated approach to restructuring. Take into account the knowledge that exists in this matter throughout the world. Military firms do not need a special form of restructuring.

Both, Western and Russian experts tend to undervalue the meaning of soft facts in management by concentrating on hard facts such as cash flow, return on investment, market share and so on. Experience from Japanese companies and their demilitarization effort after World War II tell us a different story. Which firms survived the period from 1945 to 1955 was not so much decided by the hard facts, but was positively influenced by the firms ability to.

- enhance the employees' identity with the company and encourage their commitment,
- develop and implement a long-term corporate strategy,
  enlarge progressively their business activities and the required technologies, and
- decide quickly to close-down unprofitable business units.

The successful firms were able to:

- introduce the 5-day-week ahead of all other companies,
- establish a system for a rapid market feedback, that is a professional marketing,
- quickly acquire state-of-the-art-technology, and
- establish profit centre structures.

So my third advice is: do not concentrate so much on finance and technology alone, focus your attention on management issues, planning and your staff.

Let me finish my reflections with a concluding remark about diversification, which is only one among many strategies within the broad restructuring concept, I sketched before, but which proves to be a very valuable strategy in Russia at the moment. Interestingly enough, diversification is not quite so successful in Western countries as it is in Russia: in the United States 80 per cent of the diversification projects of defends contractors ended in failure. In the whole American economy, 65 per cent of the diversifying firms leave their new market affer 5 years and 81 per cent after 10 years. In Russia this is different, because you have comparatively open markets, as far as supply is concerned. Diversification will therefore continue to be a valuable alternative, as long as the market supply pressure is low. So here is my last piece of advice: diversification will continue to be a valuable mid-term strategy. But we aware that in the long run you may undermine your technological edge by concentrating too much on diversification projects. If you do them well, they may provide cash that can be used to finance new R&D. The strategic choice will be to use them as cash generators in the mid term to nurture your core businesses to competitors. You should follow an "all or nothing at all" approach to diversification in the long run.

If you forget conversion in its old sense and make use of an integrated restructuring apporach instead, I bet, your experience will be much more positive this time.

Ladies and Gentlemen, in the limited time at my disposal I could do no more than offer a few suggestions.

For all our sakes I hope that in years to come the East-West forum will be equally frank and open.

THE CONTEXT OF CONVERSION – EXPERIENCE OF ST. PETERSBURG

Igor D. SPASSKI
General Director of
the Central Design Bureau "Rubin", St.Petersburg

In performing conversion it is very important to choose the principle of financing. In this country conversion was financed in the following way. It was decided to create a conversion fund where enormous amounts of money would be concentrated and to transfer funds from there to enterprises suffering crisis. Enterprises had to prepare business-plans or programs assuming certain commitments. Nobody paid special attention to the essence of such commitments, but companies' management declared that they would revive production within the shortest period of time, if they got funding. And the funding was provided. Concrete inspections have shown that great amounts of money were simply spent on every-day needs. There was no blocking system which could make the borrowers provide certain products for the money they got. As a rule, there was no control and generally money was spent for nothing.

It seems to me that conversion shall be financed in such a way that there could be established a kind of financial circulation. I would like to provide an example of the fishing fleet. Today this fleet has practically ceased to exist, it is worn out, it has to be revived. If plants take such orders, that costs very much. It seems natural that the state should provide the fishing fleet directly with money from the conversion fund, provided they agree that the funds are intended strictly for ordering a certain number of fishing vessels to conversion shipyards. In other words, the state shall provide funds earmarked for specific purpose. Upon getting the money from fishermen under a contract a shipyard concludes contracts with designers for vessels designing and they order required equipment. Thus, a chain of enterprises starts working on the basis of contracts. There occurs a normal financial circulation under which concrete work is done for the money got. In this case the state may expect that the funds provided to fishermen will come back from them after they get fish, contrary to other schemes according to which financial resources were just thrown away.

There is one more point of importance in conversion. In this country conversion was declared as follows: we have to fabricate products in order to fill shops with consumer goods as soon as possible. And all enterprises were forced to start manufacturing products they had never used to manufacture before. For instance, our company "Rubin" specialized in designing submarines was ordered to design equipment for fast cooking of food (dough mixers, coffee mills, etc. - in total about 50 kinds of products). Was there much sense in that? We had to hire new people, to thoroughly study the problem, ... As a result our firm has started the fabrication

W. G. Puppe et al. (eds.), Conversion of Military Enterprises, 37–40.

of such products and our defence industry with all its forces, all its 9 Ministries, has mastered the production of these 50 kinds of products according to Italian analogs. That was the end of activities in this direction. Perhaps, it would be more expedient to order this work to some enterprise of purely machine-building specialization which could develop this direction further as well.

It is very important to wisely choose the ways and methods of conversion. For instance, if it is an aviation enterprise that is of question, it evidently should develop civil aviation. Civil, passengers and other shipbuilding requires the same approach and, fortunately, they develop along the right direction. Certainly, there exist some auxiliary productions which may be mastered by shipbuilding enterprise, for instance, production of good furniture, as this technological specialization is well developed at these enterprises. The radio industry has no problems with transfer to civil production either. And small consumer goods should have been distributed more reasonably among former defence enterprises, money should have been invested in them, they should have been reconstructed and provided with technologies and so on.

Certainly, neither of us were ready to such serious processes, we had insufficient knowledge of market economy peculiarities. Active performance of conversion was suspended by such obstacles as narrow specialization, strict confidentiality, insufficient automation and informational support and many others. Inadequate psychological mood of people also played a great role. Finally, the starting conditions were of significance as well.

Why did some enterprises manage to survive and why do others die? To some extent I could get an answer to this question when I visited a number of foreign conversion enterprises, including those in the USA and France. It turned out that 50-60%, 30% in the least, of these defence enterprises' activities were focused on products hardly related to their main specialization. It is impossible to survive under market conditions otherwise. One has to stand at least on "three legs" to flexibly react to all stress situations on the market.

That was the point proceeding from which "Rubin" made decisions which have allowed the firm to remain "afloat" up to now. Such firm as ours cannot be oriented to the production of small machines for making dough or similar ones. Such enterprise shall solve serious technical problems vital for the country, those connected with the state-of-the-art technologies.

As a result of 3-years activities the firm "Rubin" managed to become the leading enterprise in designing platforms for oil and gas production in ice environment. These are cyclopic constructions of extreme complexity. Specialists in material studies, shipbuilding and power engineering take part in this work. Today several designs of such platforms have been developed. The said project entailed integration of efforts with America, England, Norway, Finland, i.e. the intensive exchange of knowledge and technologies has begun. It should be mentioned that it is not only we who gets enriched by these contacts, foreign specialists get enriched with our experience as well. Such contacts provide colossal effect in new knowledge acquiring.

The second direction of importance is stationary power engineering. Submarine-builders have experience of making compact, efficient and high-reliability power setups both nuclear and thermal. This experience has allowed the firm to develop the most interesting projects of geothermal power plants for Sakhalin and Kamchatka and to design regular thermal ecologically harmless power plants utilizing natural gas and underground atomic power plants.

About 4000 people worked in "Rubin" when reorganization started, now 1800 people work here. To keep the standards of the present time and simultaneously to survive the management of the firm had to reduce the number of personnel by half. We had to spend enormous amounts of money to equip the firm with the most advanced electronic equipment for automated design of all products manufactured, submarines included. The firm also arranged personnel training in management, design automation, finance, economy. We had to completely change the structure of the firm, to establish new departments of foreign trade, finance, organization of work, etc. Today "Rubin" is no longer the firm it was 7 years ago - in fact, today it is a holding company. All these aspects provide us with the opportunity to keep the decent level.

However, all that was done to preserve unique specialists capable of designing submarines. At present only 50% of the firm's personnel are engaged in the design of submarines. The others deal with the main topics mentioned above, but at any moment they may join defence topics and vice versa. This flexibility lets the firm maintain quite a good financial status.

But nothing of the above would have helped "Rubin", if it had not started large-scale commercial activities. About 30 subsidiaries were established around the firm and specialists from the head firm started working there for which purpose they were provided with an opportunity to get trained in new specialties. These subsidiaries had various specializations: restaurants, shops, a hotel, a business-center, a joint bank, construction, sewing, design and consulting firms. For instance, a consulting firm was established jointly with Dresdner Bank. During the first two years people suffered severe psychological problems - everybody wanted to resume his work in "Rubin". Today it is impossible to bring these people back to "Rubin". They have got adapted to new conditions, live a different life and earn good money.

It is of importance to have a good information base within the conversion process. There are about 210-215 main defence enterprises in St.Petersburg and on order of St.Petersburg Municipality our consulting firm has created a unique data base containing information on all these enterprises. The data base comprises more than 1.5 thousand descriptions of the most advanced technologies, kinds of products and various services. Everything is done by European techniques and is introduced into the informational network of Europe. First we tried to set contacts between potential partners, but then the natural process began: many companies found each other by this data base and started joint work.

And, finally, I would like to mention that all difficulties and problems of the conversion process make the personality of a firm's Director and the business characteristics of its top management extremely important for achieving success.

There must be a real team of people who can devote all their energy and time to the work, if necessary. We must look optimistically in the future, never loose heart, set new contacts, integrate in the world, look for more reasonable approaches. And everything will go on all right in our life.

CONVERSION IN RUSSIA: PRESENT STATUS AND DEVELOPMENT TRENDS

S.K. KOLPAKOV
Deputy Director
Interdepartmental Analytical Center
Moscow

The specialists in defence industry conversion usually distinguish conversion in the narrow and wide sense. Conversion in the narrow sense of the word means reorientation of defence production from military to civil products, as well as corresponding re-training of personnel. Fabrication of tractors by former tanks-manufacturing enterprises and production of civil vessels by a dockyard which earlier manufactured military ships may serve as examples of such a conversion. Conversion in the wide sense of the word implies macro-economic redistribution and adaptation of various resources belonging to defence industry – material, financial, data and human ones – with the purpose of their efficient civil use under free market economy conditions [1].

The experience of conversion in Russia and in other countries of high defence-industry potential shows that the examples of real success in performing conversion in the narrow sense are extremely rare. The conversion policy may be efficient only when the government undertakes a whole complex of steps, including institutional reorganization of enterprises, their restructuring, support of small business, transfer of dual-use technologies, training of former defence-industry managers in skills required by market economy (financial management, marketing, business-planning, personnel management, etc.), i.e. when the government handles conversion in the wide sense of the word.

A brief article hardly allows to characterize all tendencies in the process of the Russian defence industry conversion in the wide sense of the word. Therefore, the author sees his task in providing just some fragments of the general transformation process taking place today in the former Russian defence complex.

Institutional Reorganization

Changes in the ownership of enterprises having fabricated or still fabricating military products make the principle point of successful conversion and adaptation to new economic challenges. The changes mean privatization and reorganization into joint-stock companies. Out of 2000 Russian industrial enterprises which made the defence complex in the pre-reform period, 1347 have passed or undergo now the reorganization into joint-stock

W. G. Puppe et al. (eds.), Conversion of Military Enterprises, 41–46.

companies [2]. As a result the total number of former defence enterprises has split into 3 almost equal parts: governmental enterprises – 36.7 %; joint-stock companies with governmental participation – 34.0 %; joint-stock companies without any governmental participation – 29.3 % (Fig.1.).

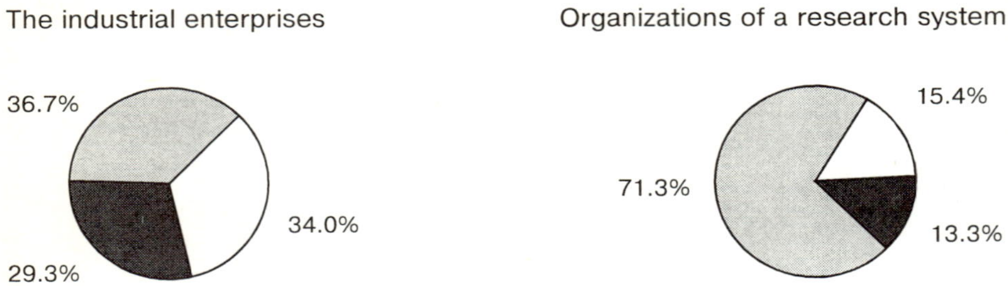

Fig.1. Present Stage of Defence Enterprises and R&D Institutions Reorganization into Joint-Stock Companies.

The same Figure provides the present-day status of the privatization process in the R&D sector of the defence industry. Here the privatization is much slower, which is quite explicable. Contrary to industrial enterprises research institutes and design bureaus of the defence complex are much more dependent on the government's support within the process of transition to market economy [3].

It is quite clear that industrial enterprises are striving to get rid of the governmental control which already for a number of years has failed to provide these enterprises with contracts, as it used to be before, or to compensate such contracts by subsidies for the support of conversion. However, it is curious that the opinion polls on the financial and economic situation conducted at a number of enterprises have given practically similar results at public and joint-stock companies. The majority of both of them find themselves in a very hard financial and economic situation, many of them are on the verge of bankruptcy [4]. In our opinion this indicates that joint stock companies established as a result of former defence enterprises reorganization have not yet become private in the full sense of this word, they present a "quasi-private" sector of the Russian economy. In such companies old traditions are still strong, the psychology of management staff and employees holding large blocks of shares has changed insignificantly.

Deepening of Enterprises' Specialization

The results of opinion polls conducted at defence enterprises prove the recent occurrence of a tendency towards the concentration of military production at such enterprises (large, as a rule), which manage to somehow increase the output of military products in spite of the general decrease continuously suffered by the military production in Russia. And the said increase in military products output is ensured rather by the growth in the

Russian weapons export, than by that in internal demand. Simultaneously the share of enterprises having no military contracts at all is constantly growing. The managers of such enterprises see the prospects for their companies development only in the civil production growth. A tendency to the concentration of military production at some enterprises and of civil production – at the others will result in establishing a smaller-size defence complex and putting a great number of former defence complex members away from this category.

Participation in the Formation of Financial-Industrial Groups (FIG)

The process of FIG formation supported by the Russian government has become quite characteristic of the recent time. At present 12 of 28 officially registered FIG's are comprised of 29 industrial enterprises and 12 R&D institutions of the defence complex under conversion. Some more FIG's having defence complex enterprises as their members are being formed now. This tendency reflects the effort of conversion enterprises to find the ways for integration of their technological and production potential into private capital which could replace constantly decreasing public funding of R&D and production programs and projects. Preconditions required for that are created, in particular, by the law "On Financial-Industrial Groups" adopted by State Duma on October 27, 1995. This law implies a number of steps to ensure the governmental support for FIG activities which is very important for conversion enterprises under the conditions of unfavorable investment climate in present-day Russia. Now a certain number of governmental regulations are being prepared. They will provide some development and addenda to the provisions of the above law in respect of privileges and allowances for FIG's [5].

Dynamics Changes in the Assessment of Financial and Economic Status of Defence Enterprises

The opinion polls of managers of various-ownership defence enterprises show that financial and economic situation of defence enterprises remains very complicated. However, the same polls prove that these enterprises have come to a turning point in their financial and economic status (Fig.2.).

The Figure shows the results of inquiries of about 150 managers of defence enterprises. Every year during four years running they were asked to estimate the financial and economic situation of their enterprises (qualitative integral assessment), every current year in comparison to the previous one. Though in 1995 the majority of managers (61 %) still mention worsening of their enterprises' situation, however, the number of those who think that their situation has not got worse (25 %) or has improved (14 %) is growing. It is for the first time since the beginning of our observations (1992) that the growth of optimistic estimations may be registered. If this trend develops next year, we shall be able to say that defence enterprises have passed the lowest point of the economic recession [4,6].

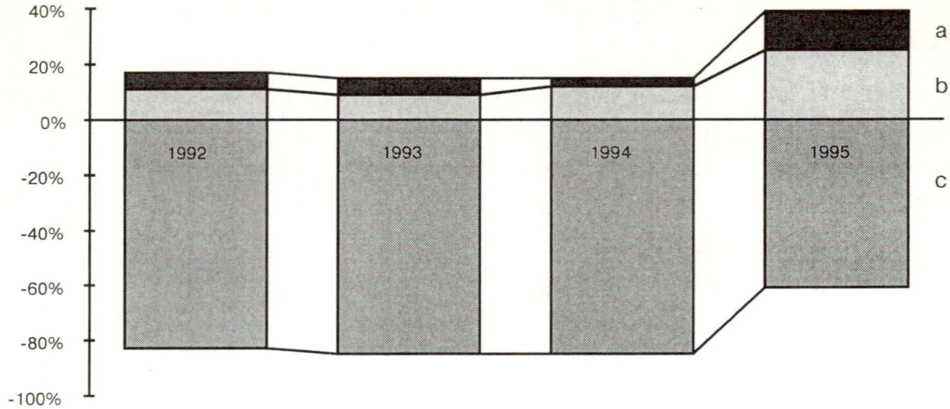

Fig.2. Dynamics of Changes in the Financial and Economic Situation of Defence Enterprises.

Structure of the Economic Recession

The conclusion on some stabilization in the situation of defence enterprises is also proved by the reduction in their civil output decline. During the period from January 1995 to September 1995 the decline in civil products output was going on in the defence complex as a whole and made 10 % in comparison to the same period of the previous year, however it is significantly less than a year ago when the figure was 33 %.

Reduction in sales of civil products manufactured by defence enterprises shows insufficient adaptation of these enterprises to solvent demand requirements, low quality of the products and warranty service and often even the loss in the competition with foreign goods not only on the international, but also on the domestic market.

However, against the background of general decline in the production of some civil products by defence-complex enterprises there may be observed some growth in certain products output. Among the latter kinds of products one should mention equipment for oil production and oil processing; technological equipment for processing branches of agricultural-production complex, trade and nourishment companies; crawler-mounted truck tractor; looms; shovels and some other.

At the same time most abrupt decline may be observed in consumer goods output. The Russian market being congested with foreign consumer goods, the domestic manufacturers of such products suffer serious crisis. Thus, the output of refrigerators during the 9 months of 1995 made about a half of the quantity produced during the same period of the last year, and that of color TV sets was reduced 4 times [6].

Strengthening of Export Orientation

Under the conditions of some economic stabilization the restrictions in demand for civil products of defence enterprises start to loosen. The results of opinion polls of enterprises managers conducted during four years show the following dynamics of changes in the demand for civil products (Fig.3).

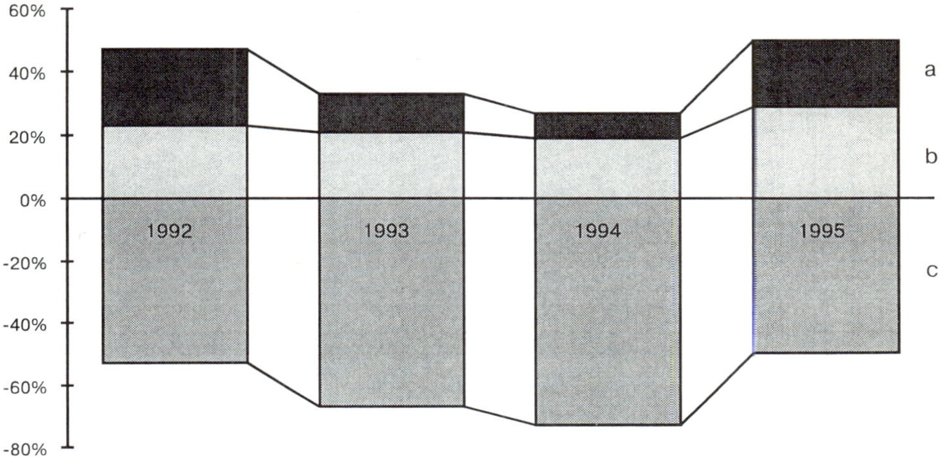

Fig.3. Changes in Demand for Civil Products of Defence Enterprises

At present about 50 % of enterprises suffer the reduction in demand contrary to 70 % of the previous year. To a certain extent this is caused by the fact that defence enterprises which used to work for domestic customers entered international market. 23 % of enterprises' managers inquired mentioned the increase in the export of civil products [7].

From the Search for Foreign Partners – to the Search for Investors.

Defence enterprises see the prospects for strengthening the export orientation of their civil products in the expansion of cooperation with foreign partners. Governmental organizations of Russia and international organizations have done much since 1992 to make project proposals of Russian defence enterprises and their technological potential known to the wide range of potential foreign partners.

The experience of the Russian-American Committee for Conversion and of other international organizations having the support of conversion cooperation as their objective shows that the process of collaboration between Russian defence enterprises and foreign partners is in its transition stage. This characteristic of the current period is determined by the following.

Just two-three years ago the main problems in the development of cooperation in conversion consisted in the search for potential foreign partners for Russian defence enterprises, in arranging a dialog between them, in presentation of project proposals and demonstration of technological potential characteristic of the Russian defence complex abroad. As a result of intensive work carried out by governmental bodies, international organizations and enterprises themselves at the present moment there are practically no sufficiently large defence enterprises which are not involved in negotiations with foreign firms on the possibility of joint conversion projects implementation. The most well-known enterprises of Moscow and St.Petersburg have more than 10 joint conversion projects under development. That brings the problem to another level – to that of search for loans and funds required for the implementation of international conversion projects. And this is the task which is very hard to solve.

Therefore, it seems to us that the main task of institutions providing support for the development of international cooperation in conversion does not any longer consist just in providing assistance to former defence enterprises in their search for potential foreign partners, but it should be an effort to start a dialogue between already formed international "teams" having promising project proposals, on one side, and institutions having funds and loan resources, on the other side.

By that I mean not only the Western capital, but Russian financial resources as well – both public and private, which may be much more efficiently used for the support of international conversion projects.

Thus, the process of former defence enterprises transformation in Russia remains complicated and contradictory, though some trends indicate the occurrence of positive changes in this field. It is quite possible that such a situation is normal against the background of those large-scale economical transformations undergone now by the defence industry in Russia.

References:

1. See, for instance: O'Prey, Kevin P. *A Farewell to Arms: Russia's Struggles With Defence Conversion.* New York: The Twentieth Century Fund Press. 1995.
2. Yu.Glybin. *Conversion of Defence Enterprises as a Component of Economic Reforms in Russia. – Military Parade*, November-December 1995. p.p.151–152.
3. V.Glukhih. *New Approaches to Defence Complex Management. – Power in Russia*, №.10. 1995. p.p.14–16.
4. *Discovery of Main Trends in Industrial Complex Development (By the Example of Defence Complex) on the Basis of Opinion Poll Among Enterprises Managers*. M.: Interdepartmental Analytical Center. 1994.
5. *Research of Financial-Industrial Groups Formation Process*. M.: Interdepartmental Analytical Center. 1995.
6. Russia – 1995: *Economic Business Conditions*, №.4. M.: Economic Situation Center. 1995. p.p.104–106.
7. D.Beljayev. *Economic Situation of Conversion Enterprises and Prospects of Their Development in 1995*: Data of Economic Situation Center.

PROBLEMS AND WAYS OF UKRAINIAN DEFENCE COMPLEX REORGANIZATION

V.A. GUSEV
Director of the Center "Orter"
Kharkov, Ukraine

The potential significance of conversion in solving the problems of reforming the economic complex of Ukraine, of technical re-equipment in civil production, of present infrastructure development, of domestic market saturation with high-quality products, of changing the export structure, of reducing power and material consumption by basic branches is stipulated by the fact that the defence complex of Ukraine (30 % of its production potential) still remains the most technically and professionally advanced part of its scientific and production complex (aircraft industry, shipbuilding, spacecraft complex, electronics, instrument making, engine building, transport, novel materials).

On the other hand, the scale of problems connected with performing controllable conversion in Ukraine appeared to be beyond its possibilities, as it surpasses even the scale of such problems faced by Russia. This peculiarity is conditioned by the fact that the defence complex of Ukraine having been deeply integrated into the all-Union one (by 70–80 %) has lost the organizational and management system adequate to its complexity as a result of independence acquired by the country.

If one takes into account that under the conditions of the deep economic crisis Ukraine has to develop the notion of its own defence strategy for the first time, it becomes clear what a knot of the most complicated organizational, financial and social problems has to be treated. It is evident that the defence complex of the country ceased to be the promising production and technological potential and has turned into a heavy burden which makes getting over crisis in economy even more difficult.

Attempts of performing conversion in Ukraine have passed several stages. In 1991–1992 the Ministry of Machine-Building, Defence Complex and Conversion was established. It was in charge of carrying out the governmental management of R&D and production enterprises of defence specialization and of arranging conversion in this sector of the Ukrainian economy. In total in 1992 this Ministry supervised the activities of 2056 industrial enterprises, 479 scientific, 246 design, 325 construction institutions, 115 trade enterprises, medical institutions, etc. As a result of uniting within the framework of a single Ministry the whole economical defence complex

W. G. Puppe et al. (eds.), Conversion of Military Enterprises, 47–53.

earlier managed by 9 Union ministries Ukraine obtained an extremely cumbersome structure which was sure to appear inefficient.

In the same years attempts were undertaken to develop a consolidated national program of conversion in the defence complex and the Law of Ukraine on conversion. Both these attempts turned out to be of no result. Instead of a single consolidated program of conversion based on priorities of military and civil production there occurred about 520 separate programs of conversion at different enterprises, the programs which were uncoordinated by both purposes and resources and presented, as a matter of fact, the attempts of directors to force their understanding of industrial policy in military and civil fields on the government. All these programs failed to fit the possibilities of the country and the majority of them died quietly at the very first stage of their implementation.

The Draft Law on Conversion was not even considered by the Supreme Soviet as by the end of 1992 – the beginning of 1993 the country entered the period of hyperinflation under the conditions of which controllable, planned conversion became out of question.

Having found themselves face to face with the problems of survival directors of defence enterprises at their own risk began to look for opportunities of utilizing the potential available: old branch contacts were revived, new forms of cooperation were established, resources were exchanged, sold, steps were undertaken to bring conventional products on the Western markets, large enterprises got cluttered up with small businesses dealing in sales of excess resources and products. However, the general tendency during these years, as well as in 1993, consisted in attempts to preserve the organizational and production structures available which found its reflection in repeated intentions and demands "to preserve the scientific and technological potential of the defence complex". It sounded exactly "to preserve", not "to reform".

In 1993–1994 the Ministry of Machine-Building, Defence Complex and Conversion and defence enterprises having accumulated certain experience of survival under the conditions of system crisis, having lost many of their illusions, including the one that the government can keep the scientific and production defence complex from destruction, began to undertake more reasonable attempts to get adapted and survive under growing inflation, unsettled priorities, leap-frog development of the Law, power crisis, destruction of the country's financial system. Initiative managers of the defence sector finally realized that they were not bound with rigid obligations to the state, that strict regulation of production activities and personal behavior traditional of military production practically ceased to exist , that they had significant production capacities and resources in their hands and the state showed little interest in them.

It was the time when conventional management elite of the Ukrainian production complex gave birth to the stratum of directors-businessmen who expressed their interest to independent mastering of new mechanisms in economic behavior. Defence enterprises began restructuring by their own initiative, they started to establish commercial banks, trade houses, holding companies, joint ventures with foreign partners, to sell and lease production buildings and equipment and so on. The active process of self-determination as owners began, though in the majority of cases this ownership was illegal, as the major part of the Ukrainian defence sector is not subject to privatization. The said processes of commercialization in the defence complex may be estimated in different ways. On one hand, reorientation in the activities of defence enterprises carried out without control by the state with regard for its interests, independent changes in the structure and character of production inevitably bring about general reduction in the technological level, loss of capabilities to manufacture many kinds of defence products, recession in the professionalism of design and production personnel, i.e. curtailing of the scientific and production potential. On the other hand, within the chaotic process of structural decay in the defence complex there spontaneously appear the elements of new economic system based on the initiative of independent persons.

Thus, conversion in the defence complex of Ukraine in many aspects develops by itself and at the same time tests this complex for survival and the ability to change according to the changes of the outward situation. I would like to emphasize once again that such processes provide strong negative consequences dramatically destroying the results of work done by previous generations, suspending for a long time whole directions in scientific, technological and production activities, misorganizing and misorienting large professional collectives. However, in these processes there occur elements promising for the future, active groups of businessmen trying at their own risk new forms of economic behavior and thus forming the need in activities coming along with their initiatives: marketing, examination, advertising, loans and other infrastructure.

Along with this spontaneous conversion efforts to perform organized conversion are still undertaken. The Ministry of Machine-Building distinguished several priority programs which allowed Ukraine to start the production of new deficit goods and products. Here are some examples:

– spacecraft complex "South Machine-Building Plant" mastered the fabrication of city electric transport, motor-blocks for small agricultural production;

– design bureau "Yuzhnoye" developed and started the production of wind-power stations;

– research-production company "Hartron" develops automated control systems for nuclear power plants of Ukraine;

– "Kiev Radio Plant" manufactures communication systems for coal industry;

– R&D complex "Kvant" masters the production of navigational and sonar equipment for the fleet;

– tank plant "Malyshev Plant" starts the production of coal mining equipment.

There are a lot of such examples. Certainly, starting new production these enterprises provide themselves with work for today and for the nearest future. Beyond any doubt, the products they manufacturer are necessary for Ukraine. However, there appears a feeling that in the majority of cases such production has no long-term prospects, that the products were chosen at random. As a rule, new production was established without preliminary professional estimations of long-term conditions on domestic and international markets, without calculations of alternative cooperation contacts, without forecasting dynamics of the economic situation in the country and many other things to be done for determining long-term orientations in production. Therefore, one may expect that already in the nearest future these (and other) variants of civil products manufacturing will suffer problems, first of all, in sales because of competition with similar products of foreign make.

During the last two years serious efforts were focused on carrying out compensational conversion when funds for conversion could be obtained as a result of military equipment sales. It is one of efficient mechanisms, though it is connected with great difficulty of entering the international market characterized by severe competition. In the nearest future Ukraine will hardly be able to get more or less significant position on this market by a number of reasons (active opposition of leading sellers of weapons, absence of various-kind political support, lack of experience, etc.). Still Ukraine began to actively take part in international exhibitions of armaments and civil equipment, thus acquiring experience it needs so badly (Abu-Dabi-94; Idex-95; Hannover-95).

The third direction in the controlled conversion consists in attracting foreign investments to modernization and reorientation of defence production. Though there are more intentions, than real results in this field. We know just few examples of direct foreign investments in defence enterprises: production of security control systems for nuclear power plant in Kharkov (Hartron-Westingaus), production of radio telephones (Kharkov, plant "Kommunar" – Federal System Group of the USA) and some others. Though the number of preliminary discussions of intentions amounts to hundreds.

The reasons for such low activity of foreign investors in the defence complex are the same as in the whole of Ukrainian industry: unsteady and incomplete law, high inflation rate, low professionalism of bureaucracy, as well as conventionally closed character of the defence sector and its extreme economical inefficiency, extreme even in comparison to other Ukrainian branches. And still it is the direction in conversion that has attractive potential opportunities for activities of mutual benefit.

First. Cooperation in the conversion of the Ukrainian defence potential makes a subject matter of some government agreements (with the USA, Germany, France) and that ensures political and some financial support of initiatives in this field by the governments of the said countries.

Second. In a number of defence branches Ukraine has first-class technologies and R&D's which may be successfully used in joint projects implementation (aerospace technologies, heavy engineering industry, power engineering included, instrument making, material studies, etc.). The best production capacities, most qualified and disciplined specialists are concentrated in the defence complex. Organizational and financial mechanisms are required for efficient utilization of these opportunities in joint projects. The main problem consists in the absence of such joint projects, the main prospects – in the possibility of their development and introduction.

Conversion in Ukraine is closely connected with the problems of reorganization in large scientific centers.

The scientific centers of Ukraine (both academic and industrial) were established as elements of a single scientific-technological complex of the Soviet Union, the fields and scale of their scientific activities were determined by the orientation of the country to leading positions in geopolitical spheres most important and prestigious for it: nuclear complex, space exploration, defence sphere in general.

The majority of scientific centers were mainly, and sometimes totally, engaged in defence topics development, as a result they had certain cooperative contacts with corresponding sectors of the defence complex and, as a rule, had very vague contacts with civil society, to say nothing about the international one.

The main problems faced by the scientific centers are as follows:

1. Ukraine has not determined its strategic purposes, in scientific and technological sphere either. Therefore, the management and scientific staff of the scientific centers have to identify themselves the prospects in scientific work. And while in applied science this may be done via the search for users of technologies in the national industry, the future of fundamental science, defence topics included, certainly, goes beyond the competence of scientific centers and requires the participation of the state. Absence of governmental scientific and technological policy undoubtedly leads to the degradation of traditional scientific fields and schools.

2. Requiring great material and power resources the fundamental science is especially critically affected by the general economic crisis and problems with power supplies. Large research setups of scientific centers are unutilized because of absence of financing.

3. The opportunities of the fundamental science reorientation to the world context as a way to ensure its support and development are very limited because of low intensity of scientific communications which, first of all, is caused by lack of state-of-the-art communication means, absence of funds for business-trips abroad and purchase of scientific data, conventional confidentiality of scientific topics.

4. The opportunity of domestic application of high technologies available and developed in the scientific centers is limited by low innovation activities typical of crisis situations, and international application is restricted by absence of culture and experience of activities on the international market of technologies, imperfection of domestic law in intellectual property protection, insufficiency of information.

5. Management structures of scientific centers earlier integrated in wider systems of activities conventionally were oriented and try to orient now to the purposes and priorities set by those system (state, branch, territory, etc.). As no target tasks are set now from outside, they shall be set from inside proceeding from the analysis and forecast of situation.

We have to agree that the majority of conventional management structures of scientific centers failed to transform in this direction, as a result they began to loose control over the situation in their institutions, which caused disintegration of research teams and brought about alternative management structures.

One of promising directions in reorganization of Ukrainian scientific centers in accordance with new reality consists in using their scientific, technological and production potential as a basis for establishing innovation structures (high-tech centers, research parks, etc.) which could gradually bring traditional scientific activities of the centers in compliance with the new requirements and opportunities in international and domestic R&D transfer.

Proceeding from the estimation of the general economic situation in Ukraine and its reflection in the scientific and technological sphere the main directions of the said institutions' activities shall be as follows:

First. Their establishing shall provide scientists working in fundamental science and high technologies with an opportunity of efficient scientific communications with world scientific and technological centers and thus shall begin the revival of international cooperation which Russia (and Ukraine) used to have up to 1930-ties and which was then cut down as a result of self-isolation of our country. For our science it seems to be the only way to prevent destruction of scientific schools, to preserve the potential and ensure conditions for its development. For the international society it is a good chance to use the scientific potential of Ukraine in international programs and projects. Therefore, the Center shall have state-of-the-art telecommunication equipment and access to world data bases.

Second. These structures shall become the place for studying international experience in stimulation of innovation processes via the implementation of governmental and regional scientific and technological policy and its adaptation to Ukrainian conditions.

Third. One of big problems in the utilization of scientific and technological potential of Ukraine, first of all, that of the defence sector, consists in the absence of modern marketing and management, developed examination institutes, legal and consulting support. Therefore, innovation centers shall implement the complex of educational and consulting programs attracting both domestic and foreign specialists for these purposes.

Fourth. The innovation centers shall ensure their economic independence via the participation in commercial implementation of their own projects or those submitted to them. So capacities shall be established in such centers for small-scale production of high-tech products and sales of these products shall be arranged.

Such work in establishing a High-Tech Center is carried out now on the basis of the National Scientific Center "Kharkov Physical-Technical Institute" which initiated the development of the international project "Kharkov Research Park".

The project is supported by governmental and regional authorities, as well as by the management of the Ukrainian municipal program "Perfection of the system to control the development of small and medium towns of Ukraine".

Such institutions as "International Incubator of Technologies" (Moscow), International Corporation of Applied Scientific Research (San-Diego, the USA), Center of Social Innovations (Vienna, Austria), a number of Ukrainian governmental and non-governmental enterprises and firms have been attracted to the development of this project. Jointly with foreign partners we study the opportunities of partial financing of the project from foreign funds (USAID, TACIS, INTAS, etc.). The grant of the NATO Science Committee has been obtained already for establishing a telecommunication center of the future research park. In the nearest future governmental decisions are to be made on stimulating the processes of establishing various-type innovation structures within the scientific-technological complex of Ukraine. That will contribute to solving main problems in ensuring legal and financial support for the processes of scientific centers reformation.

Working Session III: Different Elements of Conversion Policy (practical experiences)

CONVERSION EXPERIENCE OF RHEINMETALL GROUP AND RELEVANCE FOR RUSSIA

Hans Erhardt SCHWERDTNER
TZN Forschungs- und Entwicklungszentrum
Unterlu GmbH
D-29345 Unterl , Germany

1. Introduction

The general political situation of recent years and the economic problems which German Government and industry had to and are still faceing after unification and due to the MBFR-Treaty have resulted in dramatic budget cuts. These especially hit those companies engaged in military engineering.

Reorientation to civil products i.e. Conversion, became a buzzword! But what does is mean CONVERSION?

Conversion by definition means change, transformation, alteration. But actually conversion has to be understood as a structural change occurring within the continuous development of an economy due to various reasons.

And hence there are two opinions on how this should be achieved by the defence industry:

The first opinion is:

Conversion is a matter of – and must be guided by – the government. For this purpose the government must use budgetary monies freed due to the deliberately wanted development and treaties ratified by its politics for measures necessary to achieve a structural change.

The second opinion is something like this:

Since it has been the free decision of industry to get engaged in defence contracting it must, therefore, find through own initiative and strengh possibilities to change to civil alternate products and new fields of demand. The government has no responsibility!

In various countries the task of conversion may have absolutely different significance with differing consequences.

The question of economic significance of conversion is first dependent from the magnitude of armament and the Armed Forces of a nation in relation to its economic performance, the size of population and the degree of planned force reduction.

W. G. Puppe et al. (eds.), Conversion of Military Enterprises, 57–62.

For a nation having used a large part of ist GNP for armament and Army and having a closed military industry with millions of workers, conversion is a basically different task as for a country like Germany which spent less than 3 % of GNP for defence and had only about 1 % of ist workforce employed in the defence industry.

The question how conversion should be performed is thus dependent from the political – and economic system and the rating defence industry has within such system.

In planned economy or government-owned defence industry conversion must be much more supported by the state through planning, steering and other means.

In a democratic system with free market economy conversion must primarily be performed by industry regarding all advantages of a flexible free entrepreneurship. However, the government is asked – like with any other structural changes – to also support this process by flanking structural means.

Furthermore, the answer to the question how conversion should be handled is also dependent from whether a nation wants to further maintain reduced but anyhow modern equipped and functional forces without risking to run into a politically critical dependence from a third party.

Here the questions of independence, ability to cooperate and of military judgement play an important role.

2. The German Situation

The german situation regarding conversion is characterized by the following elements:

a) Military industry is only of low significance in relation to the overall economy.

b) Export possibilities for the german defence industry are rather restricted due to history.

c) The German Government will not get heavily engaged in the process of reduction in defence industry capacity.

d) The German Government is favourably viewing intensive cooperation with foreign part ners. However, in doing so military – and technical capabilities must be maintained.

e) Economic conditions for production in Germany became more difficult in recent years; in addition, the integration of East Germany has tied up tremendous funds.

f) Finally, the process of political – and economic integration in Europe has led to a certain relaxation of nationalistic interests.

Defense oriented companies in Germany will – in this situation – mainly find four possibilities to act which can alternatively or in combination with each other be pursued:

a) Reduction of business, production cuts according to reduced demand.

b) Alteration of production capacities for new, non-military products. This would actually be conversion!

c) Adoption of additional defence technology tasks in areas no longer covered by others.

d) Use of means to searchand secure market positions outside defence technology with out the use of existing capacities.

These alternatives are all connected with quite different risks and difficulties:

The mere **reduction of business** can generally not be an essential target for a management oriented towards growth. Especially since this reduction normally results in lower profits since fixed costs cannot be reduced fast enough.

An **alteration of production** does not solve any problems in our economy since the main assump tion for success in the market today lies in access, i.e., in marketing tasks and not in production capability.

In satiated and consumer defined markets like in German the sales capabilities determine success and especially these capabilities in the civil market are not available in defence industry.

The adoption of additional defence technology tasks may seem attractive but will normally fail because nobody is willing to surrender a once held market position just because of reduced demand.

Such adoption will, therefore, if at all only be possible by use of considerable means.

Finally, the use of means to **conquer new market positions** outside of defence industry must be understood such that

- with new products
- a success in new markets is searched.

This, amongst all possibilities of diversification has always been the most risky and difficult!

3. The Rheinmetall Route

In recent years Rheinmetall has successfully tried to respond to the problem of declining demand by a combination of these four possibilities:

Within the Holding, i.e., the Rheinmetall Berlin AG, the dependence from military contracts has – during the last 15 years – been reduced from 70 % to roughly 25 %.

In parallel, three additional business areas have been established through acquisition of respective companies:

- The Mechanical Engineering Branch, primarily through acquisition of Jagenberg AG;

- the Automotive Branch, primarily through acquisition of Pierburg GmbH;
- and finally the Office System Branch, through acquisition of the Mauser AG.

In additon to this Holding strategy the Defence Technology Branch represented by Rheinmetall Industrie GmbH has also had to face the changed market situation during the last 5 years.

Here the already mentioned combination of the four possibilities becomes especially evident:

a) Rheinmetall Industrie GmbH has, corresponding to the reduction in demand cut its traditional production almost by half. This required a drastic reduction of personnel by more than 50 %; the traditional facility in Dsseldorf was completelly closed. In sum, this has been a rather difficult and painful way!

b) An alteration in production capacities was achieved to some extent by using them to perform work farmed out as subcontract by third companies. In a similiar move our capability and facilities in the area of electromagnetic compatibility have been opened to non-military customers and an additional field was also entered with the de militarization of ammunition.

c) Rheinmetall Industrie was also able to consolidate its interests through acquisition of other defence technology companies. MAK-System GmbH has been acquired from Krupp, and Mauser Werke Oberndorf GmbH from Diehl. With these acquisitions Rheinmetall Industrie has fortified its position as The Army Supplier and increased its range of products.

d) And finally, Rheinmetall Industrie has – by using considerable funds and by acquisition of mostly small companies – gained access into new, non-military markets. These acquisitions have been made under consideration of the fact that available technical expertise could meaningfully be applied to these new tasks.

Therefore, today mainly two directions are pursued:

- For one, the industrial application of automatic image processing and pattern recognition. These applications range from quality control in production to tool positioning and control up to parts recognition and sorting.

Basic know-how from developments of so called smart munitions has successfully been transformed.

- Secondly, security technology, i.e., in the broader sense the traditional field of Rheinmetall, is now also offered in the non-military area.

Thus, automatic personnel – and baggage control is today a business field within Rheinmetal Industrie GmbH.

Of course, entering new business also requires respective adaption of existing– or creation of new organisational structures.

Contrary to military technology with its rigid product development cycle the civil market – due to reasons of competition – requires much shorter reactions and high flexibility in turning an idea into a product. In addition, there is no more one a financially sound single Z customer; everything has to happen fast and must be low price.

In this market matters: The one first earns!

And this is something companies are good at who know their market and competition since years; they can in any case do better than aone newcomer!

4. Our Experiences in Russia

The russian military industry of the past was a command guided key industry of the USSR. Therefore, it hardly had any competitor in the Soviet Union and the other East European states. The industry was monopolist with development, production and price dictated centrally by political necessities.

Due to its huge size and complex structure it was especially hard hit by the results of Perestroika, MBFR and following budget reductions.

Additionally, a shrunken home market due to autonomy of the former Republics has also let to dramatic budget cuts.

But besides natural gas and oil the export of military equipment is still viewed as a main source for foreign currency which is so desperately needed for procurement of western industrial equipment.

In this situation it is of course not easy having to consider conversion. Here support is required such as has been and still is granted for example within the frame of the EU TACIS-Program (Technical Assistance for the Commonwealth of Independent States).

As an example I would like to refer to some experiences from the LOMO and SVETLANA Project in which we participated.

These two St. Petersburg based companies with originally around 12.000 workers have been manufacturing military optics and electronics.

After a walk-through of their production facilities measures with the aim to restructure certain areas and necessary staff training have been worked out with their management.

Another part of our task was to create connections in the West in order to not only gain acces to the market but also open up possibilities for cooperations.

During this work it became evident that consulting is a necessity but that practical support is much more required.

Since this was, however, something not included in our TACIS Project it becomes understandable that the russian side was not fully satisfied with this program:

According to their opinion it does not sufficiently take into account what is – in their view – necessary to become competitive.

It is assumed that soft aid for example in management, administration, production, development, quality assurance etc. is rather less important since one could learn this from books and by training.

The advantages of russian companies are seen by their management as follows: They have highly trained workers and scientists, – compared to our standards – low wages, suitable production equipment and a tremendous, hungry market. One therefore only needs partners willing to invest – of course enormous – amounts in Joint Ventures,

This estimate of their own situation is quite often contradicting to our judgement.

One of the reasons for this certainly may be that one – convinced by the competitiveness of russian weapons technology comes to the conclusion that, therefore, also the respective producers must be competitive.

However, fact according to our judgement is that:

- the known companies are hardly an incentive for investors;
- the sometimes since Worldwar II and without modification produced, simple consumer goods like radios, refrigerators, radiators, etc. do not find buyers any more;
- too much personnel has to be taken care of otherwise;
- extensive restructuring would be required before privatization becomes possible.

It became evident that management was surprised by these completely strange necessities and would – if at all – only reluctantly accept them.

5. Summary

Successful conversion of defence industry is a tremendous task for many nation. However, significance and terms are quite different from one country to the other so that no pat solutions exist.

In Germany the situation is characterized by a largely satiated market, intensive competition, unused production capacities and open borders.

In this situation Rheinmetall has up to now found a successful answer to the altered market demands through:

- consequent capacity reduction,
- acceptance of new challenges from other markets facilitating the use of existing equipment,
- acceptance additional tasks and of products for the Defence Technology Branch
- and entry into civil markets with new products for which basic know-how was available.

This route is also generally open to russian companies. However, the particularities of the national situation and the individual companies must consequently be regarded.

INTERNATIONAL COOPERATION IN CONVERSION BY THE EXAMPLE OF BELORUSSIAN OPTICAL-MECHANICAL ASSOCIATION

V.A. BURSKI
General Director of
Belorussian Optical-Mechanical Association

It was during a long time that Belorussian Optical-Mechanical Association (BELOMO) operated within the system of the former USSR defence complex. More than 70 % of the products it manufactured were intended for special applications (space topography photographic equipment, aerial photographic equipment, photogrammetric equipment, detecting systems, sights for armored tanks, laser rangers, etc.). At the same time during the pre-conversion period 20 % of BELOMO's output fell on civil and consumer goods (photo cameras, slide projectors, some kinds of medical equipment and a number of other optical and optical-mechanical products).

The Association comprised 3 large manufacturing enterprises and a research institute, all situated in Belorussia. The management and technological structure of BELOMO complied with the conventional scheme typical of centralized governmental economy. The plants had their own foundries, machine, optical and tool shops which allowed them to ensure the fulfillment of the whole production cycle – from blanks to packaging. The number of the Association employees exceeded 20 thousand people.

That was the background against which the conversion process started at BELOMO in 1991. First, the volume of orders for special-application products decreased abruptly and rather significantly. As a result production capacities – both equipment and premises – could not be fully utilized. Simultaneously a great engineering and technological potential was disengaged. The situation was aggravated by the process of the USSR disintegration which accelerated the destruction of economic bonds between the former USSR republics.

Under such circumstances the following questions came to the foreground: What products shall the Association manufacture? How can it ensure the output it used to have? What shall it do to keep its personnel busy? After dozens of years characterized by annual increase in output, constant shortage of production capacities, absence of problems connected with products sales, with getting materials and funding we found ourselves to be absolutely unprepared to such abrupt changes.

W. G. Puppe et al. (eds.), Conversion of Military Enterprises, 63–67.

The priority of different functions fulfilled by the Association changed significantly. For a long time the main function was connected with products manufacturing. That stipulated the formation of internal relations and the staff psychology. And now products distribution or sales have become the priority and it turned out to be a great and complicated problem. At the initial stage of conversion we suffered severe material losses for lack of specialists in marketing, market analysis, sales, design, calculations and pricing under new conditions. New R&D's and their introduction to production were based on the previous experience which proved to be hardly acceptable for the work under new circumstances.

The production of consumer goods on the equipment available and by the technologies earlier used for manufacturing special-application equipment immediately brought such problem as pricing before the Association. The goods were expensive and uncompetitive. The equipment had to be replaced by a new one, but there were no funds for that. The great inertness typical of multiproduct enterprises was also a problem, as it did not allow to flexibly meet changing market requirements. All that significantly reduced the Association's capability to export its civil products and consumer goods.

At the same time the potential available provided for quite competitive technological changes in such fields as optical, casting, machining. However, potential partners were unaware of BELOMO's technological capabilities. On the other hand, we had no idea about the needs of our potential partners.

Urgent restructuring of the enterprise became of vital importance. And settlement of restructuring problems by the Association itself would have significantly slowed down the process. To ensure efficient practical steps in restructuring managers and specialists of various levels had to be trained in basic management skills required by new conditions.

The first, and not quite successful steps in conversion restructuring of production and development of competitive products revealed gaps in the theoretical knowledge and practical skills of the Association employees regarding the following aspects:

- strategic management;
- practical and strategic marketing;
- quality control;
- calculations and pricing.

Having failed to find required specialists in this country, the Association had to look for possibilities of attracting such specialists-consultants from other countries. Via different channels (governmental and private) the Association managed to take part in a number of international programs and to involve a number of Western institutions and consulting firms in cooperation. They are as follows: TACIS, "Defence Nuclear Agency", "International Academy of Science", "Education and Technology Transfer", "Grieger Mallison", "International Trade Marketing", etc.

Five manufacturing ventures have been established jointly with the following companies: "Filmann" (Germany), "Zeiss" (Germany), "Belocorp Scientific" (the USA), "Overseas Marketing Corporation" (England), "Coemar" (Italy).

In establishing JV's the Association set the following targets for itself:

- entering the international market where practically all niches have been already occupied;
- access to technologies, design;
- borrowing labor arrangements from foreign firms;
- advertising of the ventures;
- obtaining investments from foreign partners at minimum risk.

Foreign specialists conducted a number of seminars both at BELOMO and in Germany. The Association specialists were provided with an opportunity to practically study the operation of a number of Western enterprises. Consulting firms arranged meetings and discussions with a great number of German enterprises which contributed significantly to the search for cooperation projects. The consultants provided assistance in arranging the visits of specialists from more than 20 firms of Germany, the USA, England to the Association. Within the framework of the TACIS program the Association specialists got consultations and had a chance to study the work of similar foreign companies.

The Association got support in entering the international market via the arrangement of its products exhibition in Rostok (Germany) and joint development and design of products.

Along with the operation of newly established JV's BELOMO has a number of orders for direct supplies of optical elements, units, blocks and finished products to Western companies. Today more than 1000 people are engaged in both JV's and the work under foreign firms' orders and this cooperation keeps developing.

The following observations and estimations of the Association enterprises' operation made by JV's Directors are of interest:

– The general motivation to work leaves much to be desired: most often it is the work that looks for worker and not vice a versa, as it should be;

– Most of the employees are insufficiently serious about the quality;

– Infrastructure required for foreign companies operation is not developed at all.

At the same time I would like to mention some problems which have occurred within the process of cooperation with consultants:

– Theoretical data are rather of academic character, than intended for practical applications;

– Information and recommendations are given proceeding from the experience accumulated by the consultants under totally different conditions of work;

– It is desirable to have more specialists with practical experience involved in consulting activities;

– It is expedient to more widely use the principle "It is better to see once, than to hear a dozen of times". The experience proves that those specialists who have visited foreign manufacturing enterprises become more susceptible to new approaches and proposals. It is the best incentive and motivation.

– A psychological barrier in attitude to advice and recommendations given by consultants has not been overcome yet. Other people's experience is accepted with great difficulty. Very often one may feel unwillingness to get to the heart of an actual situation, an effort to "squeeze" a new situation into the framework of existing experience.

However, in general the present consulting methods provide positive effect and induce changes in mind and methods of work, stimulate search for new approaches in solving problems, whichever may occur.

Today we feel the necessity of the enterprise restructuring, of changes in its management system. A certain number of the plant's divisions have already got independence in economic activities without getting the rights of legal entities. Papers are being prepared for establishing a holding company. But the basis for solving all the said problems has always been and remains the preservation of the engineering and technological potential ensuring the production of conventional goods.

At present proceeding from its own experience of conversion restructuring in production and from that of foreign companies the Association has made maximum use of its R&D capacities in such fields as solid-state lasers, gyroscopes, complex electronic and optical units, etc. New applications of electronic and laser devices have been developed:

– laser medical equipment;

– optical security devices (security and alarm systems);

– night-vision devices and night-vision sights for civil applications;

– laser target indicators;

– technically complicated consumer goods;

– devices for environment monitoring;

– etc.

The rich and lasting experience of developing the most complicated and highest-level optical-electronic devices, availability of all technological equipment and highly-qualified engineering staff and personnel required have allowed BELOMO to start the fabrication of new products reflecting present-day international trends.

However, the problems faced by BELOMO are quite numerous:

– Focusing of attention on manufacturing military products practically did not require the development of marketing and sales facilities. Therefore, at present the shortage of dealers network and funds for advertising is critical;

– High inflation and tax rates do not allow the development of large projects which in its turn does not contribute to the full preservation of engineering and technological potential as the company has to confine its production to simple products;

– Access to catalogs of state-of-the-art element base and composition materials, coatings and paints is very limited (may be because of information insufficiency) which keeps the company from obtaining high quality and nice appearance of devices;

– It would be useful to expand the company's participation in international exhibitions abroad. Therefore, the company needs financial support for such participation or at least an opportunity of joint use of exhibition booths under share-payment terms.

– The company needs assistance in getting access to international data bases via E-mail system.

THE CONVERSION IN RUSSIA – THE LENINETZ CASE

Anatoliy A. TURCHAK
"Leninets" Holding Company
St.Petersburg

The topic of the Seminar covers both Russia and former Soviet republics. Moreover it appears to be of importance for the whole world, since at present advanced Western countries face the same or essentially similar problems.

Conversion is a very expensive task and one should get ready beforehand to realize it. But, unfortunately, the situation in the Russian Federation did not leave people with enough time for getting ready or giving much thought to the problem. As a result, enterprises had practically no time to think of new opportunities, other forms and methods of work to be able to use advanced defence technologies in absolutely new conditions both in their own interest and interests of the state.

If to talk about Leninets, in my opinion, the process taking place there cannot be called conversion; it is a process characteristic of the transition period in Russia.

Changes in the world geopolitical situation resulted in the steep reduction of purchases of the produce Leninets made for the Ministry of Defence. For example in 1990, 91.5 % of Leninets capacities were aimed at the defence industry demands. Last year this figure went down to less than 25 %. At the same time, the heads of the enterprises could not keep up with the global changes in the world, and the enterprises were not ready to present the Ministry of Defence with the technology acceptable in the context of the new military doctrine.

The latest experience taken into consideration, we have come to certain conclusions. As of now, Leninets is looking forward to the state military order and has concluded a respective agreement with the State Committee on Defence Industry under which Leninets represents a subcontractor to the Ministry of Defence and the said committee.

In response to our initiative, the State Committee on Defence Industry and the Committee on the Management of State Property permitted Leninets in 1992 to carry out privatisation and set up a holding company. Such a decision was supported by a series of measures taken at Leninets during the previous period. We must have been much luckier than many other Russian enterprises. In January 1986 Leninets, on its own initiative and being supported by the government, started as a two-tier system and stopped to be subordinate to the head organization, the former Ministry of Radio Electronics Industry. Which, in its turn, gave people an opportunity to learn to work in different conditions. First of all, new management personnel was brought up to be

W. G. Puppe et al. (eds.), Conversion of Military Enterprises, 69–73.

granted the right to deal not only with defence enterprises, but also with the state structures which could offer new opportunities to the industry and, in particular, to Leninets.

This experience allowed us to start in 1989 the restructuring of the Central Scientific-Production Department, whose management was strictly centralized. Already then, Leninets's plants and design bureaus were granted independence, however without the right to make a legal entity. In 1990, supported by the government, these independent enterprises formed a concern, which increased managers' responsibility and business activity; and the whole set of measures having been taken, Leninets got ready for privatisation by July 2, 1992.

In 1992 Leninets was transformed into a holding company. However a mere change in the name does not mean anything. Assimilation to new conditions required restructuring of the organizational and managerial system. In doing so, we had to pay special attention to accounting as well as technical control and marketing. A number of companies Leninets co-operated with provided us with much assistance. One should mention in the first place such consulting companies as COOPERS & LYBRAND and McKENZIE. Their experience allowed us to closely analyze Leninets's management system and make consistent changes in it.

At present the Leninets holding company unites 42 daughter joint-stock enterprises. The capital stock of each enterprise belongs to the holding company, which allows us, being such, to financially control the development of daughter enterprises and follow a single technical policy based on the fullest use of the available resources.

The enterprises, members of the holding company, have their own product orientation each and are subordinate to economic strategy centers. The top of each center is the Director's Board who determine the perspectives, strategy and tactics of the respective economic strategy center. As of now Leninets has 6 centers of this kind.

Positive results are achieved under the Target Planning Program. Leninets's planning system is based on the prediction and investigation of markets, partners, competitors and technology development perspectives, and thus allows us to get a clear picture of the further progress of the company. Forecasting, in this respect, should be based on the 5-year and longer-term planning, otherwise one may be left behind and miss the major tendencies in the world market and technology development. Bearing it in mind, we have set up a Strategic Investigations Center which unites highly-qualified young experts dealing with perspective analysis and prediction.

In addition, Leninets has two important public units, the Scientific-Technical Council and the Strategic Council. The members of the first council are not involved in the work of the latter, which means that a much wider range of specialists of the company take part in forecasting and progress analysis.

At present, in spite of the steep reduction of the military-oriented production from 91.5 % to 25 %, we have managed to maintain the optimal number of employees. During a period of 1990 to 1995, we had a personnel reduction of 23–24 %. Probably we should have also dismissed those people whose mentality, resources and abilities did not meet the requirements of the company. But, to avoid possible social "outbursts", the company preferred the policy of providing people with work in order they could lead more or less normal life rather than kicking them out on the street.

I would like to mention that having lost a great number of people during the last 5 years, the company would rather have one thousand or so back. Those were highly-qualified and active people who assimilated rapidly to new market conditions and demonstrated huge potential in starting their own business in the hard times of ours. To our great pleasure, a part of such specialists are coming back to the company and do have enough experience for the work in new conditions.

Having closely considered possible applications of the available resources, we determined six important sectors where the company's produce could be competitive and occupy the leading position.

First of all, it is the transport sector. Leninets used to be a designer and producer of aviation electronics; practically all domestic aircrafts, planes and helicopters, are equipped with Leninets's complex sets and systems. As we have acquired a huge experience in system design and engineering of such complex sets, our main attraction is the civilian aviation. Earlier we had not paid enough attention to this sector, whereas now we have developed the program of "conquering" the Russian civilian aviation market. And we have already achieved certain results. A new meteo radar has been designed to meet Western standards and is going to be used on all commercially produced planes. By a governemental resolution, Leninets was appointed a head enterprise in the design of a business YAK-48 airplane. In conjunction with one of Western companies Leninets is engaged in the design of a new generation of meteo radars which will not only meet, but even surpass the quality of the Western equipment presently supplied to Russia.

At the same time, the company mastered the production of various avionics components available earlier only from the republics of the former USSR. This makes the company responsible for making all parts of the civilian/transport airplane board. In this connection, two state projects have been developed. One of them is related with the development of new hypersonic technologies, the other with the design of avionics and electronics for future air carriers.

Earlier each ministry or enterprise would work only in the interests of its own sector; no close intersectoral contacts existed. Having such an opportunity today, we have considered the question of what can be done by Leninets for the fleet. Using the already gained experience, we designed meteo radars and automatic control systems for sea and river fleet as well as for harbour operation. In this respect the company has found a new application for its traditional R&Ds.

Another sector is the railway transport. During the last 5 years, we have become a reliable subcontractor to the Ministry of Railway, particularly in regard to the supply of flaw detection systems. In this field, the company occupies first place, which allows us to face our future with confidence. Today we have got requests not only from the RF railways, but also from other 19 railways which used to comprise the single railway system in the former USSR.

We also turned our efforts towards the Metro. The availability of the facilities used for the production of automatic aircraft control systems enables us to anticipate our participation in the design of safety systems for the Metro. We have signed an agreement providing for the involvement of the French company MATRA, for the renovation of St. Petersburg underground railway. Now we are considering the possibilities of our involvement in similar activities in the republics of the former USSR and CIS.

The same may be said about the ground transport. We have designed the control system for street cars and trolleybuses. This system permits electricity consumption reduction and has better ecological characteristics. The design was followed by a comparatively big number of requests from a whole series of Russian cities.

We also work in the field of automobile transport. In conjunction with the French company THOMPSON, we are developing the route computer.

The next field is radio– and telecommunications. Earlier Leninets has never been busy directly with the work of this kind. However today the company supplies the Ministry of Internal Affairs with USW radio sets which are already being produced on a commercial scale. We have also developed radio relay communication lines which are already in operation. In this field our choice fell on a specific market segment, which is related with the countryside. Unfortunately, none of foreign companies, however high their technical and production level may be, have any idea of difficulties of the Russian market. Therefore, Leninets plays the part of a locomotive in a joint effort (with a foreign company) to provide the countryside with communication facilities of all kinds. Our partner to this project is NEW BRIDGE, a Canadian company, and now we are on our way to a joint venture. We also have an agreement with Korea under which Leninets is charged with a similar job.

Another new field the company is involved in is connected with the cash flow control.

We have signed a contract with the French company CYBERNETICS for the acquisition of credit card production equipment. In addition we have developed and supplied the Leningrad region with credit card operated filling facilities. Having won a tender, the company is issued with a respective certificate; one of our plants has got quite a big request for the production of this kind of equipment next year. In conjunction with the company "Novotron", we have also designed a new payment terminal meeting the requirements of the fiscal bodies. The similar equipment being brought from the West does not meet these requirements. We consider this field of essential interest for the company, particularly regarding the possibility of using the technical resources already available.

Another important field the company is working in is ecology. We have always studied the problems related with the submarine search and have acquired enough experience in this field. The available knowledge has been aimed at the design of lab planes and helicopters which will be used for ecological monitoring in any conditions and some other purposes. Such an equipment has already been designed and recently we have signed a document on execution of works for the Ministry of Emergency Situations.

Medicine and consumer's goods are the fields where the company has already achieved much success. We have set up several joint ventures which enable us to not only provide profitability of respective production lines, but also improve the production technology. We think we need a partner here who could help us to enter the world market. Of course, practically all segments of the world market have already been occupied, and only having a reliable partner and high technologies, one may expect to get access to this market after all.

The structure of the company has to work with an allowance for existing problems, such as defaults, debts (first of all, of the Ministry of Defence) etc. To ensure the efficient work, we are looking for investments, preferably Russian investments. For example, we already enjoy the support of St. Petersburg Promstroybank in the development of our prospective fields.

In addition, the company has formed its own financial bloc and set up financial structures, including a Stock Center, a Future Stock Exchange, a Medical Insurance Company, a Pension Fund, a Real Estate Company and an Audit Company. These structures are quite successful. Their tasks assigned by the company are aimed at such a distribution of their profits which could provide investing and first of all investments in R&D and engineering.

Unfortunately we have now arrived to a point when the available production equipment is getting out of date. That is why, within the framework of its 5-year planning system, the company provided for the measures aimed at the replacement of equipment.

However, people are of greatest importance. If there are no specialists who can head each kind of activities, the conversion process control will be impossible. In this connection, the company pays much attention to educational matters. For example, it has concluded a series of agreements with St. Petersburg State University, St. Petersburg State Technical University and the Academy of Instrument Engineering and Automatics. Of value is the creation of a special department at which the students have their classes only three or four days per week, the other 2 days they work in holding companies, being paid both their scholarship and salary. As a rule, the second-year studends start working in laboratories and on graduating from the university they come back to the same groups they used to work in. There also exists a post-graduate department which provides out highly-qualified specialists. This year the competition to enter both the special department at the Technical University and the post-graduate department is rather high.

In addition, jointly with an American company, we have set up an educational center, the Company Competitiveness Development Center, which is going to retrain specialists from Leninets as well as anybody interested from St. Petersburg and the Northwestern region.

However, an idea that the situation at Leninets is ideal and fully OK would be wrong. We suffer the same problems any Russian company currently has. Maybe it is slighly easier for us, because the most difficult period for the company is already over. We are sure that within 2 to 3 years our company will have a good position not only on the domestic market, but also on the markets of the world.

MILITARY CONVERSION IN THE CIS – A CONSULTANT'S VIEW

Merco de NORONHA
British Aerospace Consultancy Services Ltd
620-622 Birchwood Boulevard
Birchwood Warrington Cheshire WA3 7QW

I. Introduction

I am a Director of British Aerospace Consultancy Services which is a centre of consultancy expertise at the heart of British Aerospace Plc (BAe) and I would like to give a Consultants view of some of the challenges of military conversion and offer a few practical recommendations. My remarks will be challenging and I would like to focus on the practical issues rather than the theory.

As many of you will know, BAe is one of Europe's largest manufacturing and exporting companies. BAe is an international major player in defence and commercial aerospace – two sectors which have undergone dramatic restructuring in the last four years. BAe has had to dramatically restructure and re-engineer not only its corporate structure but also its manufacturing operations to achieve levels of production and cost competitiveness undreamt of only a few years ago.

It should not be forgotten that BAe was formerly a state-owned organisation and has direct experience of privatisation and that when talking to military industries in the CIS we speak from hard won practical experience.

BAeCS was a consultant on the 1992 TACIS Defence Conversion Programme and established Defence Advisory Groups in Kharkov, Minsk and here in St.Petersburg.

The first problem which has to be addressed is that the term "Military Conversion" is vague, ambiguous and highly symbolic – it is assumed to be a "good thing". However, in reality it is highly contentious and there is no agreement about what it means and what it is trying to achieve.

2. The Challenges of Military Conversion

For example. Figure I shows just a few perspectives which will be familiar to most of you. You may sympathise with some of them and strongly oppose others. But each one has its own appeal. It depends where you are standing.

W. G. Puppe et al. (eds.), Conversion of Military Enterprises, 75–81.

QUESTION: WHAT IS DEFENCE CONVERSION: ANSWER: NO AGREEMENT

Is it ... ?

- Economic aid to promote political stability
- Defence capacity reduction
- Opening up new markets for western business
- Creating competitive new enterprises
- Protecting employment
- Industrial espionage
- Safeguarding western political interests
- A fast buck for western consultancies
- Economic strategy games for western bureaucrats

Figure 1 – What is Defence Conversion?

The problem for the consultant Is that this unresolved "disagreement " is then fed into a contractual relationship between the beneficiaries and the funding agencies both of whom are subject to external pressures.

CONFLICTING OBJECTIVES

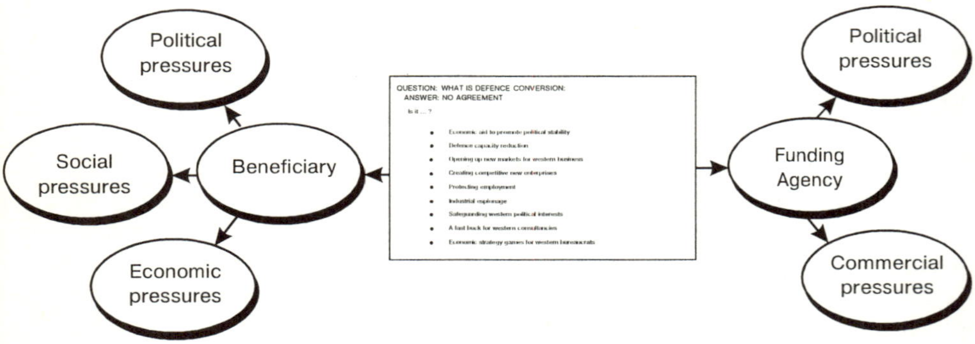

Figure 2 – Conflicting Objectives

The beneficiary inevitably faces political, social and economic pressures – for the managers of a military industry there is no such thing as a purely commercial decision. Meanwhile the funding agency attempts to reconcile the political and commercial elements of its own agenda. Clearly there is plenty of scope for suspicions and misunderstandings between them and they can soon find themselves pulling in opposite directions.

To this is added a second contractual relationship – the consultant, who is employed by one side to provide services to the other.
The consultant has a dual role.

THE CONSULTANT'S DILEMMA

- Beneficiary's advisor vs. Funding Agency's advisor
- Technical expert vs. Commercial broker
- Recommend tough decisions vs. Not directly responsible for consequences
- Fulfil terms of reference vs. Meet actual needs

Figure 3 The Consultant's Dilemma

CONFLICTING EXPECTATIONS

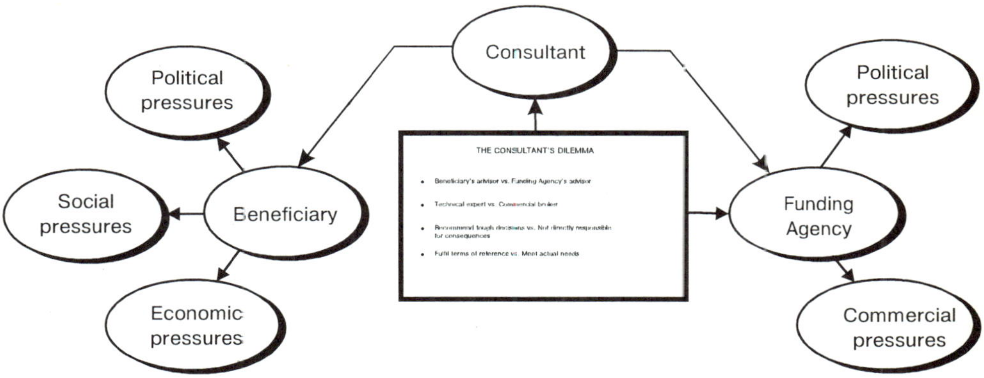

Figure 4 – Conflicting Expectations

The consultant may well find himself pulled in two directions. He has to choose between his paymaster or his beneficiary. Some consultants may think "So what! That is what technical assistance is all about! The problem is enormous; anything you do will just be a drop in the ocean. Just take the money and do what you are told. Don't worry too much if it doesn't work!"

We do not agree. In our view technical assistance is about achieving real, tangible and sustainable results on behalf of the beneficiaries. The critical "deliverables" are not the consultant's reports. The critical "deliverables" are commercially viable enterprises.

3. Two Approaches to Military Conversion

So how **do** we create those enterprises? There are two approaches.

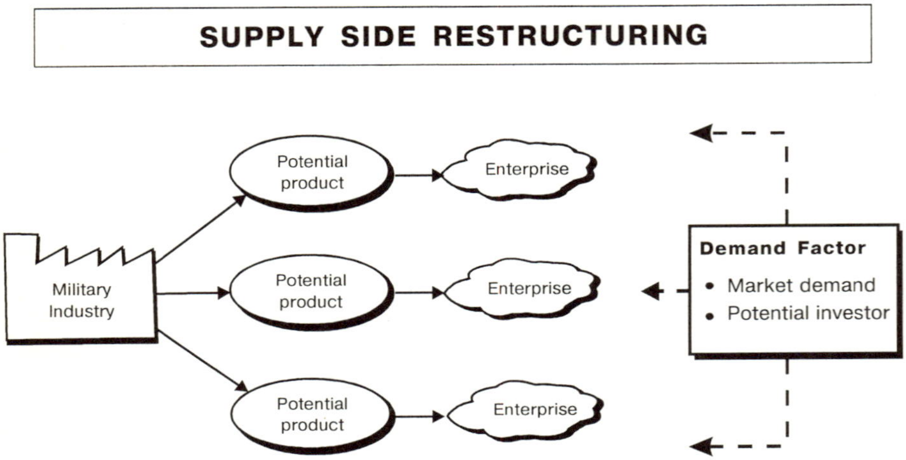

Figure 5 Supply Side Restructuring

I have called the first one "Supply Side Restructuring" but it may also be described as the "Political Approach" .

- The first step is to examine the existing supplier – the military industry – by conducting a comprehensive asset identification.
- The second step is identify what it can produce – this may be a new product or it may be an existing one. Of course there is no point in doing this without undertaking a comprehensive market analysis and preparing a sound business plan.
- The third step will then present itself. Simply take those hard decisions...downsize, re-engineer and before you know it you are in business.

It is bound to work – on paper – but in practice the chances of success are limited. Supply Side Restructuring relics on assumptions at each stage.

- The first assumption is that without any clear incentive and simply because the Defence Conversion Programme requires it the military industry will comply with the asset identification, market analysis and business plan.

- The second assumption is that the managers will be able or prepared to take these difficult decisions without the support of clearly identified investors or partners.
- And this brings me to the third assumption – that the pre-conceived plan is so good that investors and partners will either turn up somewhere along the way or won't even be necessary.

You may be able to tell that I have my reservations about this approach.

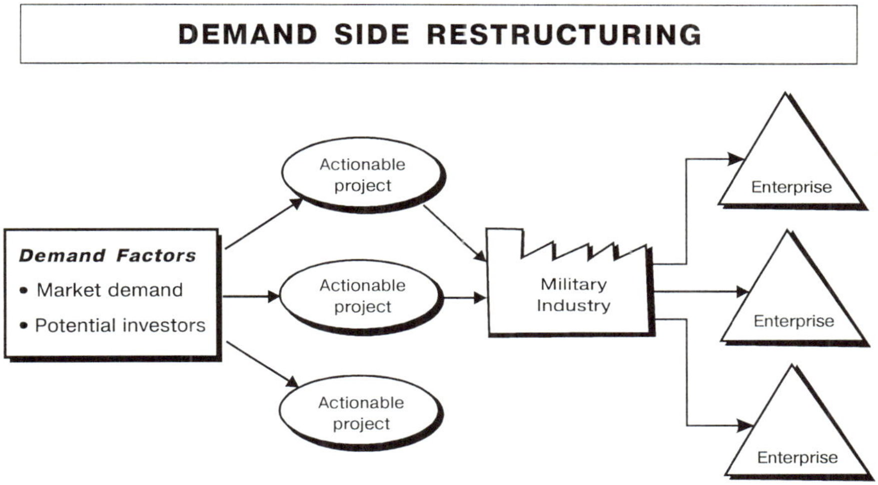

Figure 6 Demand Side Restructuring

I have called the second approach "Demand Side Restructuring" but it might also be called the "commercial approach". This is the recognised route to commercial recovery.

- It acknowledges that the demand factors are critical and regards the Identification and bringing together of market demand and potential investment as the first step of the restructuring process. Demand factors include local consumer demand, government procurement and import substitution policies and the investment strategies of international investors. The military industry's project is to satisfy market demand and a reliable way of achieving this is by establishing business partnerships with potential investors – often the most suitable investors are western companies looking for an agent, representative office or Joint Venture through which to manufacture under licence or commence distribution in the region.

Once an achievable project has been identified and the industries and their potential partners have a clear idea of the actual restructuring requirements they are then in a position to assess one another and make an informed judgement on the scale and distribution of the probable risks and benefits of the venture. This puts the industries in a position where they are able to persuade their own external influences of the acceptability of restructuring.

4. Key Principles – Long-term Vision, Relationships and Flexibility

In our experience Demand Side Restructuring is the more viable approach but it relics on the crucial assumption that the Defence Conversion Programmes is built on the key principles of long-term vision, relationships and flexibility.

Restructuring is a long-term process in a fast changing environment. The participants must have long-term vision and a willingness to respond to changing needs. There is no quick fix. Many beneficiaries will have already had bad experiences of western consultants who have turned up, asked a few very sensitive questions, written a report and then simply got on the plane and gone home. It is easy to understand why some industrialists have developed "consultant fatigue" and why they are reluctant to co-operate with a consultant unless they are confident that the consultant has the commitment , the expertise and the professionalism to deliver successful results. The consultant must establish his legitimacy. Under the TACK 92 Programme the beneficiaries had very little involvement in the selection and appointment of the consultants. The legitimacy of the consultant was established by the funding agency. Once deployed the consultant's first task was to build a relationship with the beneficiary to reaffirm this legitimacy and establish an understanding of the beneficiary's needs. Speaking for ourselves, we did this – but it took time. It also underlined the discrepancies between the actual needs and the terms of reference.

The consultant also has to establish his credibility with the potential investors. When it comes to investing in former military enterprises western businesses proceed with caution. From their point of view the commercial risk is immense. They have an Ingrained suspicion of military Industries In the CIS and they also bear in mind that a consultant based in the CIS has his own interest in getting enterprises off the ground – "has he gone native?" The consultant has to establish his legitimacy on this front as well.

During this time the consultant plays a key role in establishing trust between the potential partners and maintaining the momentum. This long-term process could conflict with the budgeting procedures of the funding agency.

In our experience and in the experience of companies like ourselves the programme management style of most funding agencies is remote and bureaucratic; prescriptive rather than responsive. But flexibility is critical to successful change management.

5. Practical Recommendations

I am conscious that I have spoken at some length about the obstacles to successful Conversion Programmes . I would now like to recommend a few simple measures to take better advantage of the opportunities.

5.1. IMPROVE PROGRAMME PLANNING

- Reduce the time between project identification and project implementation. The sort of delays suffered by the TACK 1992 programmes meant that in a number of projects the Terms of Reference were obsolete before the consultant even arrived. Here in St. Petersburg, for example, the beneficiaries' requirements had changed significantly.
- Parties must accept that the process is long-term, and the continuity of projects and relationships is critical to the success of a programme.
- Do not underestimate the logistical obstacles to success. Military industries are often situated in remote locations where telecommunications facilities are unreliable, equipment is difficult to procure and access to information is limited. Programme plans and budgets should take these factors into account.

5.2. IMPROVE PROGRAMME MANAGEMENT:

- Quicker decisions.

  The way in which programmes are often planned and structured subjects decisions to unnecessary delay and restrictions. It is not unknown for important initiatives to grind to a halt whilst the in-country team awaits the appropriate authorisation – such delays can undermine the credibility of the programme. Quicker decision-making is essential.

- Decisions made by in-country team.

  The most effective way of releasing programmes from their bureaucratic shackles is to transfer the decision-making authority to the in-country team.

British Aerospace Consultancy Services remain optimistic that Defence Conversion Programmes can achieve successful results and deliver viable commercial enterprises but in future we will only work on programmes where the Demand Side approach is accepted and the management recommendations outlined have been adopted.

WITHIN THE CONVERSION PROCESS

Oleg G. SOKOLOV
Deputy General Director
of the Central Research Institute "Prometey",
State Scientific Center of the Russian Federation

My presentation will be focused on some aspects of conversion in science, in particular, on the example of the State Scientific Center "Prometey". Two years ago about 60 Russian scientific institutions out of 4000 candidates were awarded the status of the "State Scientific Center" and that determines the level of scientific activities conducted by such State Scientific Centers (SSC).

The SSC "Prometey" was established in 1939 as the first and at that time the only institute dealing in the development of special kinds of armouring. It was armouring for tanks, planes, ships and during the Second World War the quality of Russian armouring became well known all over the world. After the war the institute became subordinate to the Ministry of Shipbuilding Industry and later worked mainly in two fields: shipbuilding industry and nuclear power engineering. The institute conducted activities in some other fields as well, but in the said ones it occupied the leading position in our country.

Till 1990 the major part of "Prometey"'s R&D's were in materials and high technologies for military equipment. After 1990 the quantity of these R&D's decreased abruptly. It seems natural that, as a result, the company should have ceased to exist, but nothing of the kind happened. This year, like before, the company's portfolio of orders is 100% full. If there is anything that worries the institute management, it is the unsteady financial position of customers which fail to timely do their payments.

Today the factor of switching to different fields in companies' activities has become the most important one in our country and all new programs adopted at the federal level - both military and civil - require that R&D's should be of dual use.

In fact, during all the years of its existence "Prometey" was engaged in what is called now by the popular word "conversion". For instance, when the institute developed new materials and high technologies for military shipbuilding, it simultaneously developed materials and technologies for civil shipbuilding as well.

Since the first days of its operation the institute has worked with something which is now called "dual-use technologies". First of all it is nuclear power engineering, production of high-strength steels and titanium alloys. Regarding nuclear power engineering I can say the following. Like "Prometey" has been engaged in everything related to the technology of transport military reactors since the moment when the first

W. G. Puppe et al. (eds.), Conversion of Military Enterprises, 83–85.

atomic submarine was created, similarly the institute has been the leader in developing materials and technologies for atomic power engineering since the moment when the first atomic power plant was established. Today utilization of atomic reactors waste has become the task of general human importance for the whole world. "Prometey" is developing a program of work in this most important field.

The institute's R&D's in special high-strength steels find new applications in drilling platforms for oil and gas production in the shelf districts of the Northern seas, in atomic ice-breakers and modern high-speed vessels.

Finally, special attention should be paid to the fact that in the world today all power resources on the territories of continents have got more or less exhausted or are coming to an end and the work on the deep-water shelf begins. And, in fact, R&D's of "Prometey" will be used in the exploitation of Sakhalin and Shtokman shelf fields which will begin in the next century. These R&D's will provide for obtaining quite a high economic effect. For instance, it has been calculated that the application of superhigh-pressure pipes of new high-strength steel at Shtokman field will allow our country to save about 2 billion dollars. This list of examples of direct conversion of military R&D's into civil ones is far from being full.

The next aspect of great importance for fundamental R&D's is titanium alloys. These materials may be considered as the ones of the next century because they feature the absolutely unique combination of strength, "eternal" corrosion resistance, nonmagnetism and other attractive characteristics. Here also Russia traditionally has been the leader, however, that was true only for the military field, as until recently there were practically no civil applications of titanium alloys.

It should be mentioned that potential opportunities of titanium alloys production in Russia are higher than in the rest of the world. But it is because of conversion that now the application of these unique materials has dropped practically to zero both in the USA and in Russia. If before 1990 the main quantity of titanium alloys was consumed by the aerospace industry and military shipbuilding and a small quantity was used by other industries, then in the next century this ratio could be changed and the said remarkable alloys could be efficiently used in civil fields. Moreover that now a number of countries, first of all Norway and the USA, develop the projects of using equipment of titanium alloys for the depths more than 300 m. In other words, everywhere where occurs the vital problem of equipment repair and revival the application of titanium alloys may put repair and revival work away for dozens or even hundreds of years. However, there exists a kind of psychological barrier, not only in Russia, preventing titanium alloys from wide introduction into economic activities.

Today rapid changes take place in the field of novel materials and high technologies all over the world. First of all there appear amorphous materials featuring absolutely unique characteristics; intermetal materials; intellectual materials which can remember the whole program preset by a designer and later reproduce it in operation; high-temperature superconductivity; ultradisperse nanophase materials; materials for bioenergetics. And quite naturally all these fundamental R&D's cannot find immediate commercial application.

To understand what approaches to solving this problem there may be one has to consider the aspects of financing. First and foremost, I would like to reassure our potential investors by saying that foreign investments is the last thing we intend to use. However, we are not going to isolate ourselves from the world community, especially now when we have entered the international society "MRS" - the largest material studying society among those existing in the world. A Russian branch has been established on the basis of "Prometey" and Academician I.V. Gorynin, the General Director of "Prometey", is the first President of this society.

We understand that our R&D's may be used on commercial basis as well. But still in the USA and in other Western countries special state federal financing is provided in this field. It is very difficult to do without that until a fundamental R&D acquires commercial character. By our estimation about 30% of R&D's shall be financed by the state.

The major part of fundamental R&D's (about 70%), certainly, shall get funding on commercial basis. And in this field Russia, unfortunately, has neither experience, nor possibilities, as banks and commercial companies do not invest in science and technology, they invest only in trade. Therefore, it is necessary to change the Law in such a way that investments in fundamental and commercial R&D's may become not less profitable than, for instance, in trade. Then everything will get in the right place.

CONCLUSIONS AND RECOMMENDATIONS OF THE SCIENTIFIC-RESEARCH SEMINAR "CONVERSION OF DEFENCE INDUSTRY — PRACTICAL APPROACH FROM THE POINT OF VIEW OF SCIENCE AND INDUSTRY"

Analysis of the practical experience of conversion in the Russian Federation provides for the following conclusions:

- Conversion presents a specific form of defence industry restructuring;
- Conversion is a long and expensive process;
- Conversion processes in the Russian Federation are closely connected with the general structural crisis in the Russian economy;
- The Russian Federation has no strict state policy of conversion, conversion processes take place without any system, sometimes in an uncontrolable mode, with low efficiency;
- Several Russian enterprises have accumulated positive experience in conversion, this experience shall be studied and disseminated.

The conversion problems are of international significance. At the same time the importance of conversion and terms of its performing are different in different countries, therefore, there may be no universal solutions in this field The scale, terms and rate of conversion in the Russian Federation, absence of balanced market economy make the use of Western experience under Russian conditions impossible.

The participants in the seminar consider that conversion in the Russian Federation requires complex and coordinated activities of the state, regions and conversion enterprises. One-sided efforts will be of no success.

To make the situation more steady and to increase the efficiency of conversion in the Russian Federation the participants in the seminar recommend the following steps.

At the federal level:

1. To formulate the concept and state policy in conversion. They shall be based on the defence doctrine and well-founded defence order.
2. To intensify the work in the formation and implementation of federal programs related to conversion activities proceeding from their connection with international conversion programs and international agreements of the Russian Federation. The said programs shall be oriented to establishing the reserve of high-efficiency technologies, dual-use technologies and to selective support of priority defence branches and production.
3. To increase activities in certification of conversion products and evaluation of intellectual property.
4. To expand the application of mechanism for the support of conversion products manufacturers by providing conversion funds to the buyers of such products.

W. G. Puppe et al. (eds.), Conversion of Military Enterprises, 87–88.

5. To implement the policy of reasonable protectionism in foreign-trade activities to stimulate the following:
- import of investments instead of finished products;
- export of finished products (export of armament included) instead of raw material and fuel.

At the regional level:
1. To increase the coordination in conversion activities on the basis of establishing regional informational centers and consulting-introductory infrastructure.
2. To take conversion processes into consideration in the development and implementation of regional industrial policy.
3. To promote the systems of municipal orders and programs with due regard for conversion activities.

At the level of conversion enterprises:
1. To take a complex approach to restructuring starting from the development and implementation of enterprises' long-term strategy.
2. To master new non-military products only in case there is actual market demand for conversion products, innovations and dual-use technologies.
3. To expand the application of the diversification strategy, to establish funding sources on the basis of diversification projects to support main activities, technological level and new R&D's.
4. To establish profit-centers at optimum decentralization, to arrange and stimulate establishing of business "incubators" on the basis of enterprises.
5. To actively utilize in conversion advantages and potential of new organizational-legal forms of business activities (financial-industrial groups, scientific centers, etc.).
6. To perform conversion with full consideration for organizational-management and labor aspects, introducing new adequate management methods and structures and carrying out personnel retraining.
7. To improve planning and management of conversion programs in cooperation with foreign consultants and investors.

The participants in the seminar recommend to proceed with business meetings and contacts between the countries of the West, the CIS and Russia in the field of conversion policy.

Participants

Mr. Konstantin ALDEV
Consul-General
Consulate-General of the Bulgaria Republic
Phone: +7-812-273-69-69
Fax: +7-812-272-57-18

Mr. Alexander ALEXANDROV
Director General
Association of St. Petersburg Industrial Enterprises
Phone: +7-812-251-40-03
Fax: +7-812-251-49-34

Mr. Igor BAKHMETYEV
St.Petersburg Mayor's Office
Deputy Chairman of the Committee for Economy and Finances
Phone: +7-812-319-93-60
Fax: +7-812-319-96-22

Mr. Konstantin BEZVIKONNIY
Director
Bremer Vulkan Verbund AG, St.Petersburg
Phone: +7-812-296-08-46, +7-812-296-47-49
Fax: +7-812-296-68-87

Mr. Arseniy BEREZIN
Director General
SANTA-BARBARA Joint Venture, St.Petersburg
Phone: +7-812-534-13-63
Fax: +7-812-552-13-30

Mr. David BERNSTEIN
Research Associate
Center for International Security & Arms Control, USA
Phone: +1-415-723-21-86
Fax: +1-415-723-00-89

Mr. Emile BLANC
Chairman
Western European Armament Group
France
Phone: +33-1-4442-51-72
Fax: +33-1-4442-57-68

Mr. Ratmir BOBOVIKOV
NORTH-WEST Association, St.Petersburg
Chief of Department
Phone: +7-812-274-68-75
Fax: +7-812-110-0040

Mr. Ivan BORISAVLJEVIC
Foreign Expert, Project Manager
EU TACIS Programme Co-ordinating Unit - Belarus
Phone: +375-172-76-80-61
Fax: +375-172-27-25-15

Mr. Evgeny BOZHENOV
The Russian Federation State Committee on Defence Industry, Moscow
Assistant to First Deputy Chairman
Phone: +7-095-972-78-90
Fax: +7-095-251-97-82

Mr. Vyacheslav BURSKI
Director General
The Byelorussian Optical and Mechanical Association, Belarus, Minsk
Phone: +7-0172-64-11-90
Fax: +7-0172-63-75-57

Mr. Vladimir DATSKO
President
National Institute of Enterprise, Moscow
Phone: +7-095-392-75-49
Fax: +7-095-393-98-14

Mr. Klaus DOMINIK
President
Akademie der milletstandischen Wirtschaft, Germany
Phone: +49-30-632-80-09
Fax: +49-30-632-80-09

Mr. Vasiliy EGOROV
Vice-President
International Informational Academy (Baltic Branch), St.Petersburg
Phone: +7-812-218-40-87,
Fax: +7-812-218-37-87

Mr. Alexey ELYASHEVITCH
Director
Department of Science and Higher Education at the St.Petersburg Mayor's Office
Phone: +7-812-278-11-60
Fax: +7-812-278-18-27

Mr. John M. EVANS
Consul-General
USA Consulate-General
Phone: +7-812-275-17-01
Fax: +7-812-110-70-22

Mr. Anatoliy FATEEV
Deputy Manager
PROMSTROYBANK, St.Petersburg
Phone: +7-812-271-29-35

Mr. Marcello FAVARETO
Project Director
FATA Engineering & Contracting
Italy
Phone: +39-11-966-86-15
Fax: +39-11-966-13-46

Mr. Andrei FURSENKO
Director General
St.Petersburg Regional Foundation for Scientific and Technological Development
Phone: +7-812-394-35-83
Fax: +7-812-394-78-87

Mr. German GARDYMOV
General Director
Production Company SEVERNYI ZAVOD, St.Petersburg
Phone: +7-812-246-19-65
Fax: +7-812-239-74-26

Mr. Lev GIK
Director General
Kaliningrad Regional S&T Center, Kaliningrad
Phone: +7-0112-27-31-07
Fax: +7-0112-27-31-07

Mr. Boris GLADKIH
Chairman of the Industrial Policy Committee
St.Petersburg Legislative Assembly
Phone: +7-812-319-92-87
Fax: +7-812-310-52-19

Mr. Yuriy GLYBIN
First Deputy Chairman
State Committee for Defence Industry of the Russian Federation, Moscow
Phone: +7-095-251-97-82, +7-095-972-79-66
Fax: +7-095-251-97-82

Mr. Alexey GORIGLEDZHAN
Head of the International Marketing Administration
BALTIYSKIY Bank, St.Petersburg
Phone: +7-812-315-30-81
Fax: +7-812-310-92-74

Mr. Eugeniy GORIN
Director General
St.Petersburg Industry Support Foundation
Phone: +7-812-271-07-86
Fax: +7-812-319-99-35

Mr. Jose Maria GRANDA COTERILLO
Project Manager
ISDEFE
Spain
Phone: +34-1-411-50-11
Fax: +34-1-411-47-03

Mr. Gennadiy GRISCHENKOV
First Deputy Director
Central Research Materials Institute, St.Petersburg
Phone: +7-812-271-28-88, +7-812-278-93-02
Fax: +7-812-110-76-60

Mr. Gerhard HUBRICHT
TZN Forschungs und Entwicklungezentrum Unterlug GmbH
Germany
Phone: +49-5827-87-619
Fax: +49-5827-56-39

Mr. Sergey IVANOV
Deputy Chief of the Defence Industry Department
Committee for Finances and Economy at the St.Petersburg Mayor's Office
Phone: +7-812-319-93-18

Mr. Alain H. JUBIER
Director for International Programs of Science Committee NATO
France
Phone: +32-2-728-42-28
Fax: +32-2-728-42-32

Mrs. Marina KALASHNIKOVA
Researcher
Institute of the USA and Canada of Russian Academy of Science, Moscow
Phone: +7-095-280-48-36
Fax: +7-095-243-91-68

Mr. Alexander KENNAWAY
Eur. Ing. Professor
Conflict Studies Research Centre
England
Phone: +44-1276-41-23-46
Fax: +44-1276-68-68-80

Mr. Georgiy KEZLING
Director
Central Research Institute for Economy and Conversion of Military Industry, St.Petersburg Branch
Phone: +7-812-186-28-33
Fax: +7-812-252-94-65

Mr. Henrik A.E. KONARKOWSKI
Managing Director
A/O KONVERSULT
USA
Phone: +1-910-659-74-50
Fax: +1-910-659-75-64

Mr. Vladimir KOPCHENOV
Deputy Director
The Krylov Shipbuilding Research Institute, St.Petersburg
Phone: +7-812-127-93-48
Fax: +7-812-127-93-49

Mr. Nikolai KORABLEV
Deputy Technical Director
ALMAZ Shipbuilding Joint-Stock Company, St.Petersburg
Phone: +7-812-350-01-71
Fax: +7-812-235-70-69

Mr. Anatoliy KOROLEV
Director General
ALMAZ Shipbuilding Joint-Stock Company, St.Petersburg
Phone: +7-812-235-51-48
Fax: +7-812-235-70-69

Mr. Alexander KOVTUNOV
Adviser of the Chairman of SCMTP of the Russian Federation,
State Committee for Military-Technical Policy of the Russian Federation, Moscow
Phone: +7-095-220-18-42

Mr. Jochem KREHER
Senior Associate
PSB GmbH, Germany
Phone: +49-30-6953-36-86
Fax: +49-30-635-09-78

Mr. Alexander KREPAK
President
Regional Development Foundation, St.Petersburg
Phone: +7-812-278-10-00
Fax: +7-812-278-12-91

Mr. Alexey KUDRIN
First Deputy Mayor of St.Petersburg, Chairman of the Committee for Economy and Finances
St.Petersburg Mayor's Office
Phone: +7-812-315-51-52
Fax: +7-812-319-92-92

Mr. Samuil KUGEL
Director
International School of S&T Sociology, St. Petersburg
Phone: +7-812-312-64-54
Fax: +7-812-218-41-72

Mr. Valentin KUZNETZOV
Director General
Central Research Materials Institute, St.Petersburg
Phone: +7-812-271-49-72
Fax: +7-812-110-76-60

Mr. Gunnar LARSEN
Managing Director
NORODIN AS
Norway
Phone: +47-73-52-24-50
Fax: +47-73-51-40-90

Mr. Yves LOISEAN
Consul-General
French Consulate-General
Phone: +7-812-312-93-02
Fax: +7-812-312-37-25

Mr. Thierry MALLERET
Counsellor
European Bank for Reconstruction and Development, United Kingdom
Phone: +44-171-338-61-58
Fax: +44-171-338-61-11

Mr. Jean-Louis MOYNOT
Vice President
France Conversia, France
Phone: +33-1-44-95-36-47
Fax: +33-1-44-95-36-98

Mr. Hanns Peter MUTH
General Manager
Enterprise Plus Ltd.
United Kingdom
Phone: +44-442-870-391
Fax: +44-442-870-345

Mr. Vladimir NICKOLTSEV
Director General
Central Research Institute GRANIT, St.Petersburg
Phone: +7-812-271-67-56
Fax: +7-812-274-63-39

Mrs. Albina NIKKONEN
Director General
St.Petersburg
TRAINING-CENTER Ltd.
Phone: +7-812-394-78-87
Fax: +7-812-394-79-51

Mr. Merco Johan James Amilius de NORONHA
Executive Director
British Aerospace (Consultancy Services) Ltd.,United Kingdom
Phone: +44-1925-822-337
Fax: +44-1925-822-483

Mrs. Nina ODING
Deputy Director
LEONTYEVSKIY CENTER - International Social-Economical Research Center, St.Petersburg
Phone: +7-812-319-91-00

Mr. Henning von OERTZEN
Merges & Acquisition
W+ST Undternehmensberatung GmbH
Germany
Phone: +49-30-721-80-53
Fax: +49-30-725-189

Mr. Valentin PASHIN
Director General
KRYLOV Central Research Institute,
St.Petersburg
Phone: +7-812-293-54-82
Fax: +7-812-127-95-95

Mr. Vladimir POPOV
General Director
SVETLANA Joint-Stock Company,
St.Petersburg
Phone: +7-812-554-03-70
Fax: +7-812-553-70-01,
+7-812-553-37-01

Mr. Eduard POTIOMKIN
Director General
TRANSMASH Central Research
Institute, St.Petersburg
Phone: +7-812-135-98-50
Fax: +7-812-135-98-37,
+7-812-146-16-18

Mr. Wolfgang G. PUPPE
Direktor Osteuropaprojekte
DOWC Ost-West-Consult,
Germany
Phone: +69-263-72-30
Fax: +69-263-72-50

Mr. Valeriy RADCHENKO
Director General
ZVEZDA Joint-Stock Company,
St.Petersburg
Phone: +7-812-262-80-05
Fax: +7-812-267-46-85

Mr. Uwe ROPER
Vice President
Radian Corporation, Canada
Phone: +1-403-283-23-77
Fax: +1-403-270-74-40

Mr. Eduard RUTKOVSKIY
Deputy Director
Central Research Institute
for Economy and Conversion
of Military Industry,
St.Petersburg Branch
Phone: +7-812-186-90-93
Fax: +7-812-186-90-93

Mr. Vladimir ROSTUNOV
Chief of the Department for International
S&T Programs of General Administration
for Armament, Conversion and Utilisation
of SCMTP of the Russian Federation,
State Committee for Military-Technical
Policy of the Russian Federation,
Moscow
Phone: +7-095-220-18-42

Mr. Vadim SALMIN
Director
Samara Science-Co-ordinating Center,
Samara
Phone: +7-8462-33-91-47
Fax: +7-8462-32-11-53

Mr. Dmitriy SERGEEV
President
Association of St.Petersburg
Industrial Enterprises
Phone: +7-812-310-05-05
Fax: +7-812-113-48-25

Mr. Carl-Hans SCHLUE
President
BNP-Dresdner Bank
Germany
Phone: +7-812-312-30-92
Fax: +7-812-312-20-22

Mr. Hans Ehrhardt SCHWERDTNER
Director
TZN GmbH, Germany
Phone: +49-5827-87-669
Fax: +49-5827-53-56

Mr. Oleg SHULYAKOVSKIY
Director General
BALTIYSKIY FACTORY Joint-Stock
Company, St.Petersburg
Phone: +7-812-217-10-79
Fax: +7-812-217-22-96

Mr. Michael SIEBERT
Stellvertretender Generalkonsul
Generalkonsulat der Bundesrepublik
Deutschland,
Phone: +7-812-273-55-98,
Phone: +7-812-273-57-31
Fax: +7-812-279-32-42

Mr. Grigoriy SLABIKOV
Chief
Federal Administration for Enterprises
Insolvency and Bankruptcy,
St.Petersburg
Phone: +7-812-276-16-65
Fax: +7-812-276-11-55

Mr. Oleg SOKOLOV
First Deputy Director
Central Research Institute
for Construction Materials PROMETEY,
St.Petersburg
Phone: +7-812-274-25-08,
+7-812-274-10-32
Fax: +7-812-274-17-07

Mr. Alexander SOLOVEYCHIK
Director General
LENPOLIGRAFMASH Joint-Stock
Company, St.Petersburg
Phone: +7-812-234-24-20

Mr. Igor SPASSKIY
Head and Chief Designer
Central Design Bureau for Marine
Engineering RUBIN, St.Petersburg
Phone: +7-812-113-51-32,
+7-812-314-37-69
Fax: +7-812-164-37-49

Mr. Sture STIERNLOF
Consul General
Sweden Consulate-General
Phone: +7-812-218-35-27
Fax: +7-812-213-71-98

Mr. Pavel SYKHOTA
Vice-Consul
Poland Consulate-General
Phone: +7-812-274-41-70
Fax: +7-812-274-43-18

Mr. Johann A. STANDER
Consul
South African Consulate-General
Phone: +7-812-325-63-63
Fax: +7-812-325-63-62

Mr. Anatoliy TURCHAK
President
LENINETZ Holding Company, St.Petersburg
Phone: +7-812-264-32-19
Fax: +7-812-299-90-41

Mr. Sergey TZIPLYAEV
Representative of the President of the Russian Federation in St.Petersburg, Representatives of the President of the Russian Federation in St.Petersburg
Phone: +7-812-274-70-21

Mr. Alexander VASHETS
Scientific Secretary
Russian Mobile Vehicle Engineering Institute Joint Stock Company, St.Petersburg
Phone: +7-812-135-93-79
Fax: +7-812-135-98-37

Mr. Anatoly VORONJUK
Chief Engineer
LENPOLIGRAPHMASH Joint Stock Company, St.Petersburg
Phone: +7-812-234-19-31
+7-812-234-11-83,
Fax: +7-812-234-23-16

Mr. Mark VYBORNOV
Minister
Ministry of Foreign Relations of the Leningradskaya Oblast
Phone: +7-812-278-55-87
Fax: +7-812-274-59-86

Mr. Charles WINNINGTON-INGRAM
Consul
Consulate-General of the United Kingdom
Phone: +7-812-325-60-36
Fax: +7-812-325-60-37

Mr. Zurab YAKOBASHVILI
Deputy Minister,
Ministry of Science and Technological Policy of the Russian Federation, Moscow
Phone: +7-095-229-47-74
Fax: +7-095-230-28-23

Mr. Valentin ZANIN
Director General
SIGNAL Research&Manufacturing Association
Phone: +7-812-567-22-33
Fax: +7-812-567-83-55

Mr. Alexandre ZAKHAROV
General Director
Production Association
"KALININ Works", St.Petersburg
Phone: +7-812-350-13-54
Fax: +7-812-352-57-35

Mrs. Natalia ZOLOTYH
Deputy Director General
TRANSTEHCNOLOGIA Patent-Licence Firm, Moscow
Phone: +7-095-250-15-37,
+7-095-250-09-39
Fax: +7-095-250-41-87

Agenda

Day 1: Monday, November 20th, 1995

8:00 Registration / Coffee

10:00 **Opening Plenary Session:**
A. Kudrin, Deputy Mayor of St. Petersburg
A. Jubier, NATO Program Director
Z. Yakobashvili, Deputy Minister for S&T Policy of Russian Federation
D. Sergeev, Co-Director of Workshop
W. Puppe, Co-Director of Workshop

Working Session I: Conversion in a Changing World

10:30 J. Glybin, Deputy Director of Goscomoboronprom (Moscow)
"Conversion of Enterprises in Russia"

11:00 D. Bernstein, Stanford University (USA)
"Key Lessons of Conversion Experience 1986-1995"

11:30 Coffee Break (until 12:00)

12:00 E. Blanc, Foundation France Conversia (France)
"French Experience with Military Conversion"

12:30 Th. Malleret, EBRD
"The Policy of EBRD towards Military Conversion and Restructuring - Programs and Projects"

13:00 Lunch (until 14:00)

Working Session II: Structural Conversion of Industry

14:00 D. Sergeev, President of the Association of Industrial Enterprises (St. Petersburg)
"Industrial Crises: Reasons and Solutions"

14:30 W. Puppe, Dresdner Banc Group, DOWC Ost-West-Consult, Director (Germany)
"Concrete Experience with Conversion and Restructuring Projects"

15:00 I. Spassky, General Director of RUBIN (St. Petersburg)
"The Context of Conversion - Experience of St. Petersburg"

15:30 Coffee Break (until 16:00)

16:00 **Round-Table Session I** (until 18:00)

Topics:

1. Implementation of Effective Conversion; Methodology of Decision-Making; Approaches and Techniques; Evaluation of Forecasting Methods and Trend Indicators to Determine Conversion Priorities
2. Government Contracts - from Preparation to Implementation
3. Peculiarities of Conversion in Regions with a High Scientific-Technical Potential
4. State Stimulation and Guarantees for Private Investment at Federal and Regional Levels
5. Direct Financial Regulation
6. Indirect Financial Regulation
7. Creation of Industrial Enterprises and R&D Centers with Different Forms of Ownership as a Way of Diversification of Large Concerns
8. Policy of Demonopolisation

19:30 Departure at Reception

Day 2: Tuesday, November 21st, 1995

Working Session III: Different Elements of Conversion Policy (practical experiences)

9:30 H. Schwerdtner, Rheinmetall Group (Germany)
"Conversion Experience of Rheinmetall Group and its Relevance for Russia"

10:00 A. Turtchak, General Director of company "Leninetz" (St. Petersburg)
"Conversion in Russia - the Leninetz Case"

10:30 D. Cabagnols, Thomson CSF (France)
"Program Rosunikom - a Joint Russian-European Project"

11:00 Coffee Break (until 11:30)

11:30 V. Burskiy, General Director of BELOMO (Belarus)
"Conversion Experience with Western Consultants"

12:00 M.J.J.A. de Noronha, British Aerospace Consulting Services Ltd. (United Kingdom)
"Military Conversion in the CIS - a Consultant's View"

12:30 O. Sokolov, Deputy General Director of PROMETEY (St.Petersburg)
"Promotion of the High-Tech Potential in the Process of Conversion"

13:00 Lunch (until 14:00)

14:00 **Round-Table Session II** (until 17:00)

Topics:

1. Influence of the Federal and Regional Government Agencies on the Formulation of Science and Technology Policy
2. Government Science and Technology Programs: from Preparation to Implementation
3. Establishment of Scientific Production Units to International Standards in the Context of Conversion
4. Support of Innovation through New Forms of Ownership and the Establishment of Foundations and Techno-Parks
5. Protection of Employment as a Factor of Economical Recovery
6. The Role of Consultants in the Conversion Process
7. Retraining of Skilled Workers
8. Valuation of Investments in New Enterprises in the Form of Intellectual Property

18:00 Departure to the Theatre (Bus)

Day 3: Wednesday, November 22nd, 1995

9:30 Departure to the Enterprise ALMAZ, St. Petersburg, (bus)

Working Session at the Enterprise ALMAZ

12:00 Departure to the Congress-Center

13:00 Coffee-break (until 13:30)

13:30 Concluding Discussion (until 15:00)

15:00 Closing of the NATO-ARW

Day 4: Thursday, November 23rd, 1995

Business Meetings

Index